Twice *as* Good

Twice *as* Good

Leadership *and* Power *for* Women *of* Color

DR. MARY J. WARDELL

NEW YORK

LONDON • NASHVILLE • MELBOURNE • VANCOUVER

Twice *as* Good
Leadership *and* Power *for* Women *of* Color

Published in New York, New York, by Morgan James Publishing in partnership with Difference Press. Morgan James is a trademark of Morgan James, LLC. www.MorganJamesPublishing.com

ISBN 978-1-64279-630-8 paperback
ISBN 978-1-64279-631-5 eBook
ISBN 978-1-64279-632-2 audio
Library of Congress Control Number: 2019907438

Cover Design by:
Rachel Lopez
www.r2cdesign.com

Interior Design by:
Bonnie Bushman
The Whole Caboodle Graphic Design

Morgan James is a proud partner of Habitat for Humanity Peninsula and Greater Williamsburg. Partners in building since 2006.

Get involved today! Visit
www.MorganJamesBuilds.com

This book is a dedication
to the memories of
my mother, Mary Eliza,
and my father, James,
whose lives and leadership made
my life and dreams possible.

**This book is written for
powerful women of color
who lead themselves
and others every day.**

I am not afraid to be black as midnight
  Gold as pollen honey
  Red as cinnamon
  Sepia brown or cinnamon red
    Yellow
    Red
    Sepia
    Kola
    Cinnamon
I am not afraid to be hungry
I am not ashamed of the curve of my behind
I am not afraid to be hated
I deserve to love myself and give this love to others without fear of rejection
I am not afraid to be joyful
I am not ashamed to be proud.

  – **Janice Mirikitani**, poet and activist

Table of Contents

Foreword

Dr. Mary J. Wardell's book written with depth of experiences, understanding, and intelligence provides for us women of color a strong voice that opens up the silences that have muted our own voices, stories, and sense of worthiness–indeed our power to lead.

We are a country of dreamers. How tragic that in this nation of diverse populations, purported equal opportunity and access to its established institutions, injustices and inequality persist in the most pernicious ways. The barriers that feel impenetrable for people of color—specifically women of color-especially in the work place and many arenas where racism and misogyny are practiced—have become so sophisticated in their institutionalization, that these structures have become the accepted "norm."

We have faced over these past decades—and particularly in the past three years–a country divided and torn by self-interest and greed. We experience and witness a vast number of poor and middle-income people fearful of losing basic rights to health care, food, and housing security. We live with an administration blatantly permissive to white supremacists and racist hate crimes; one that has mocked, disrespected, and demeaned women, and has terrorized an entire nation of new and undocumented immigrants, and even naturalized citizens. The tremors of unrest and protest grow, and with them we see the rising up of women and a wave of women of color, who more than ever, are running for more national political offices—with the chants of women's marches, #MeToo, #TimesUp, Black Lives Matter movements and young people protesting against gun violence as the encouraging wind at their backs.

San Francisco's own Mayor London Breed is a shining example of a woman of color, who was raised in poverty and the "projects" of the black community, and who has risen to succeed and lead a major city.

Dr. Wardell's *Twice as Good: Leadership and Power for Women of Color* is a great resource book of our stories. We are privileged to hear from a woman of color who has succeeded as Vice Provost of a major university, who has served on city commissions and agencies, and who knows the dangers, the challenges, and the unspoken requirement to be twice as good, working twice as hard as her white counterparts... men and women. Intuitively, Dr. Wardell feels the perception of women of color having to be twice as good, as she has struggled with her own internalized pressures, and those of other women. She understands the necessity to define her own self, to trust her judgment of actions and strategies, and not allow the inbred negative stereotypes about women of color to distract her. She understands the power of us telling our stories— those which have damaged, diminished, endangered ... and restored us. She also provides important information about how women of color need to affirm their power with community, with encouragement from empathic circle of friends, and with equity of access.

As Co-Founder of GLIDE Foundation, I have worked for 54 years with my husband, Rev. Cecil Williams, to build one of the largest nonprofit service and spiritual organizations in San Francisco. Our programs are comprehensive and have expanded to provide wrap-around support services for thousands of people who come to us with myriad of needs, including free meals, shelter, recovery, family support and childcare, counseling, and training programs. As an Asian American woman, I can tell you my story which has resonated with many of the women of color I have worked with. Gaining recovery from my history of childhood incest, past violent relationships, a deep sense of unworthiness, and feeling undeserving of love, I realize it is the power of story which has saved my life, and continues to remind me that recovery, forgiveness, and loving one's self is a lifelong journey. And perhaps my most difficult lesson has been that I must claim and enact my power, not isolated or entitled, but with the people I purport to serve and love. My experiences at GLIDE have taught me that change begins with one's self, and the values of respect, unconditional acceptance, and love of all people no matter what our differences, must become the culture of organizations and of society. We must touch the hearts and minds of people in order for them to believe they can change the circumstances of their lives; and help make a difference in the lives of others who need innovative opportunities to break the cycle of oppression. "Social justice for all" are meaningless words if we do not embrace a culture of respecting the complexities of what it means to succeed—one size does not fit all. Women of color have and continue to experience the difficulties of overcoming racial, gender diminution.

Ironically, women of color have always been powerful. They have illumined the path to freedom from slave plantations. They have survived concentration camps with dignity and perseverance. They have nurtured new immigrant children in hostile communities. They have raised us to be who we truly are, with all the rich cultural and racially powerful steel in our backs. It is America who has not recognized this power, and continues to undermine the ways in which people of color and women particularly can truly break through the ceilings which limit our possibilities.

Dr. Wardell's wisdom is needed now more than ever, to solidify our determination to build community, to open ourselves to hearing each other—especially through our disagreements—and trust in our connection that we can be—twice as powerful.

—**Janice Mirikitani**, poet and activist

Introduction

In the spring of 2015, Michelle Obama gave the "Twice as Good" speech to the graduating class of the historically black institution Tuskegee University in Alabama. Tuskegee, which was created by Booker T. Washington in 1881, has graduated leading professionals from all walks of life including politicians, scientists, entrepreneurs, and educators among others. Washington, in the September 1896 issue of *The Atlantic*, speaks about his personal quest for an education and about his desire for Tuskegee Institute graduates to be an example for fellow African Americans, on "how to lift themselves up" thanks to their education.

Mrs. Obama said, "The road ahead is not going to be easy. It never is, especially for folks like you and me. Because, while we've come so far, the truth is that those age-old problems are stubborn and they haven't fully gone away. So, there will be times when you feel like folks look right past you, or see just a fraction of who you really are."

In spite of the reality of an uneven playing field with deeply embedded structural racism, where poverty and unemployment penalize the African American community, Michelle Obama understood that she, and the new university graduates sitting before her, would not be given a pass. She told the graduates, "I want to be clear that those feelings are not an excuse to just throw up our hands and give up. They are not an excuse to lose hope. To succumb to feelings of despair and anger only means that in the end, we lose. The world won't always see you in those caps and gowns. They won't know how hard you worked and how much you sacrificed to make it to this day," she continued, "instead they will make assumptions about who they think you are based on their limited notion of the world."

She went on during her commencement speech and told of her concern about how she was perceived during her husband's presidential campaign. She worried about the effect that those perceptions might have on her daughters. In the end, she decided to concentrate on being twice as good, a philosophy she has embraced since her college days.

———

For years, African American parents have repeated to their children that they must be twice as good in order to succeed in a world rampant with racial discrimination. I heard the same in my home and in my church as a child growing up. You must be twice as good to achieve half as much as others. Over time, I would learn that the "others" were white Americans. While the truth underneath the message didn't sound very positive or fair, the lesson itself was probably one of the few strategies available to Black parents in their attempt to prepare their children for a better life and for what they would inevitably face on their path to that better life.

Considering that the landmark United States Supreme Court case Brown v. Board of Education of Topeka, 347 U.S.483, did not come about until 1954, how many other strategies were available to families, educators, and clergy to combat structural and societal inequity? Brown was a critical step forward but it certainly didn't even up the playing field from centuries and decades of exclusion, violence, and repression for men and women of color.

Progress is being made, yet hasn't come about quickly. For women of color in the professional workplace, progress has been slow as a whole. Thus, the "Twice as Good" lesson became an instrument or tool for negotiating the reality of a situation. Twice as Good was a methodology consciously employed by generations of African Americans passed down from parent to child for resistance to obstacle in the face of great racial injustice.

This book is a disruptive leadership framework on being unapologetically yourself at work. This book is written for women of color who want to be taken seriously as leaders without having to seek approval from others. *Twice as Good* is for women of color who dare to show up as their truest self, with joy and resolve, in the face of barriers which are real and sometimes invisible. *Twice as Good* is for people who are transformative allies to those women.

Through intimate storytelling, *Twice as Good* seeks to empower all women to excel in their lives and careers. Having worked with a range of women across diverse fields for decades, I recognize that now is the time for women of color to step into their power. Conscious of their distinct identities and lived experiences and their inclusive leadership, I affirm women of color as strong, courageous, and capable leaders that they are.

———————

This is a pivotal time in our nation. With a booming economy and low job unemployment rate, the gender disparities in leadership roles across positions and industries are growing instead of closing. There is a dismal percentage of women serving as directors on corporate boards persists. The State of California alone has 84% of its corporate entities out of compliance in this area. Disparities across health, education, housing, environmental, and financial outcomes between those who benefit from the prosperous economy and those who continue to suffer persist.

Women of color are needed today, perhaps more than ever before, to step into their power and assume their leadership.

We need their commitment to an ideal of society rooted in a purpose greater than the individual. We need their love for communities beyond their own and a sense of care for people. We need their ideas, insights, and perspectives to reframe entrenched and embedded problems with new solutions. We need their hope, knowing that things must improve today for a brighter tomorrow.

This leadership framework is developed as a model and guide for preparing women of color to become leaders ready for their next major opportunity so that when it is presented, they are ready to step in.

How women of color lead are making the news and people are paying attention. In the political realm, we are witnessing how Stacey Abrahms in Georgia, Kamala Harris in California and Washington, D.C., to Alexandria Ocasio-Cortez in New York City, each show up with purpose in their leadership. Unfortunately, some underestimate their brilliance yet we see that their purpose is to address and create economic, social, and political value in the marketplace and work environments from a place of social justice and inclusion. This book is a call to action for women of color to take bold forward movement, in their own way, within their leadership trajectory—African American, Latina, Indigenous, Asian American, Pacific Islander, and other minority women whose excellence demand our attention. As a diversity scholar, higher education executive, and educator, I care about the organizational cultures and the spaces women of color find themselves. This work locates the progression of women of color within the context of institutions and organizations. These places are social and cultural structures that can either propel or suppress women of color at work.

Through intimate storytelling and personal reflections, *Twice as Good* urges women of color to tell their personal narrative as they prepare for work life in industry or the public square. To tell your personal narrative means you must be able to live it out loud, in a meaningful and trusting manner. Traditional notions of workplace identity that rewards conformity misses out on the ingenuity and specialness that women of color bring each day. This is a problem in the modern workforce and that must change for all people.

Gender inequity and misogyny within organizations are toxic realities for women of color. Any organization or societal impediment that takes a woman of color further away from her true self needs to be challenged and amended for her sake and everyone else's. By challenging the status quo, she can fully realize her leadership to improve workplace performance and societal outcomes. The key focus in this perspective is the intersection of gender and race and the unique ways in which that dynamic intersectionality shows up every day for women of color.

One of the primary things I have done in *Twice is Good* is share my experiences, lessons learned, failures, and successes over time. Through telling the truth and being vulnerable about gender and race in the American workforce, I share principles of leadership transformation for women of color and areas of personal development critical to stepping into power on their terms.

It's at the intersection of gender and race where women of color find themselves most impacted as leaders in the workplace and in the world. Conversations around gender, particularly gender and leadership, are often reduced to sexism at work. Gender inequality in the workplace is a serious problem that demands our attention. Yet we tend to not fully understand what the challenges are that people of color encounter in organizations when they experience both sexism and racial inequality. We are better at doing something about blatant forms of discrimination. The popular 'lean in' strategy is a good start for empowering women to assert themselves in a gendered environment, yet women of color must push harder and farther than their male counterparts and white female colleagues. The challenges they face are unseen and invisible.

For women of color who lead or who want to, the work environment is like navigating troubled waters. You find yourself in difficult waters that are unseen by others yet known and felt by other women of color. You need to proceed with caution and strength; intelligence and courage; to withstand and push through the currents of racism and sexism together in full effect.

This work acknowledges culturally-informed understandings that reside within women of color urging them to access wisdom that has been passed down through generations. Our cultures, often through our mothers, are grounded in wisdom and knowledge. I share stories of how my mother passed her wisdom to me. The link to my own journey of leadership and power is extended to the reader as a communal embodiment of sharing, as a gesture of love that was passed on and given to me, from her mother, and so on.

Understanding who I am, through my mother, propels me toward greatness that is difficult to describe yet a firm grounding that all springs forth. That realization gives me the confidence and courage to engage and confront the most perplexing and difficult challenges in my life. Confronting inequality and the reality of exclusion is part of the experience of women of color in America. Doing something about inequality and inequity is the legacy of women of color in America. There is a legacy of resilience and overcoming hegemonic and racist acts and the institutions that perpetuate them and the systems they dwell within. While leadership and power is in the DNA of women of color, there is a discovery process each individual must engage to uncover and understand the greatness that lies within. As a mother, partner, and executive, I continue to uncover the mystery of who I am, all the while, unleashing confidence from knowing that I already have everything I need.

I am gifted, female, and Black. And that is everything.

This book acknowledges the different realities in the workplace women of color experience and how they navigate micro-aggressions and macro-aggressions and other forms of racism with resilience and grace. I continue to encounter women of color who are masterful in negotiating passive yet aggressive situations with integrity and love. Some are able to maintain a traditional career trajectory in confronting the gender inequity and racism in corporate roles and continue excelling as they move through promotions. Yet, far too often I have witnessed women of color will pay a price for speaking up and telling the truth for the good of the organization and its' mission. A diminished career trajectory with promotions that go to peers with lesser technical knowledge and preparation is a far too common reality that organizational leaders recognize as a systemic failure and form of institutionalized racism. This all too common circumstance needs to change. In my experience working with women of color, these unfair situations are an opportunity to be mindful and take charge of what happens next in their lives.

Twice as Good is a counter guide to annul the interplay of race and gender in the American workplace. Women of color will confront challenges and roar beyond the hegemony and misogyny to discover and own their power.

―――――――――

"Wade in the Water": A Metaphor for Challenge and Strength

I grew up singing in the Black Church and the Negro spiritual "Wade in the Water" was one of many songs that was a part of the music lexicon of my faith and cultural heritage. Looking back, I can't help but ask myself,

"How do three-, five-, or nine-year-olds learn how to move like water, in a perfect rhythmic motion like that while they sing?" I can remember how everyone in the church was in physical and spiritual sync as we sang this song in community.

The only reasonable answer for me is that there was something visceral, something resonant, and something real that had been transferred and learned from that Wading in the Water experience that was passed on to me, passed on to the other black children in my church community, and passed on to the community that descended through African ancestors.

When we sang "Wade in the Water" in church, I remember how everyone would begin to clap their hands and we would sway back and forth in a flowing movement. As we worked through the verses, our sway would become even more rhythmic and pronounced as if we, too, were having an emotional experience of wading in the water ourselves. I loved the feeling I had when our voices crescendoed and we emotionally took on the journey of mimicking what it might actually feel like to wade.

In my cultural heritage, enslaved ancestors were following an intricate secret code system of communication offered in the words of songs in the form of spirituals that gave freedom seekers clues, directions, warnings, and encouragement. I was singing a secret code song that would change the course toward freedom for the singers themselves.

The journey was for those who were bold, faithful, and strong enough to fight through the oppression and the dangerous passage through the Underground Railroad. "Wade in the Water" was a metaphor for personal leadership, determination, and strategy filled with information about how to find and get to safe passage. It was a navigational song on how to outmaneuver and anticipate the captor's ill-intention. It was a song of hope, strength and encouragement. It was a song about how to face your fear. It was a song about having faith when all odds are working against you.

If we knew how to sway and move our bodies to "Wade in the Water" without being taught how to do so, we also retain within our consciousness lessons of hardship, resilience and leadership from our ancestors that can inform and accelerate our power in the modern workplace. This is just one song of many like them. It took me years to recognize that my ancestors had passed on instructions to me, they gave me codes with specific directions, they left me clues on leadership and strategy that would help guide me on my own executive leadership pathway as a university dean, a vice provost, mother, wife, teacher, community leader, friend.

———————

For women of color who lead or who want to, our work environment is like navigating troubled waters. The key is to recognize when you are in difficult waters and know what to do to be effective in your work. You will be strong and courageous to withstand and push through the repressive current with the support of others and the awareness that you have all the tools available to work through the repression.

When you face challenge at work, "Wade in the Water" is a metaphor for you to use. The difficulty women of color experience with others at work often stems from other people's fear about what a woman of color's success and growing leadership means for them. This creates what I call the invisible force that goes beyond a form of competition. The invisible force for women of color at work is a state of passive yet unrelenting environmental struggle and opposition that create unforeseen setbacks for her success. Not adversarial or outwardly hostile behavior, yet void of the qualities of partnership or advocacy for her growth and development. The promise of allyship is still too far away for her.

I found the words of "Wade in the Water" are also a balm to sooth doubt or discouragement when the odds are stacked heavy and high. As a leader, it's an artistic expression of a strategic summons to faith, hope, and strength. The great abolitionist, anti-racist leader, and women's rights activist, Harriet Tubman accompanies courageous participants into the troubled waters, recognizing their anxiety and fear, yet leading them against and through invisible and visible currents. You, too, embody the capacity to enter, engage, and exit the most troubling of situations at work and beyond. Part of the work is to connect to the wisdom and knowledge of ancestors in your own heritage and tradition and pay closer attention to lessons, codes, strategies they've already passed down.

This intention is to build your awareness to know the cultural asset and wealth that exists inside as you move into positions of power. This is important for leadership development to know and understand your strengths. Bringing moral clarity into your work that emerges from direct experiences with inequality is a strengths-based leadership approach.

Women of color bring moral clarity into the workplace. You are called to leverage the intersection of gender and race as a leadership advantage and gift to the world that only women of color can manifest and give to others through their culturally informed lived experiences.

Support and Empowerment

The book is to support and empower you who are working hard and making a difference for others through your jobs. I want you to know that you matter. My hope is to reflect parts of your narrative as I share my own story and the reflections of other women of color. I want you to feel connected to others who see you and understand you, united in the challenges and opportunities you experience in the workplace.

I draw upon 25 years of experience as an executive leader and share what I have learned along the way. There are real pitfalls that women of color must know about. And there are real advantages that only being a woman of color brings. The intersection of gender and race is specific and threatening in traditional organizational environments.

Through narratives, interviews, and reflections, I share lessons I have learned in one of the most traditional and hierarchical fields in the country, higher education, and the emerging challenges for women of color working in modern industries like technology. As a leadership educator, my work is to accompany women of color as they ascend to where they are meant to be; whether an early career professional, a mid-level manager, or C-suite executive.

This leadership framework is an opportunity to document my experience and share with others. There is tremendous power in putting down in writing what you have learned and how you have changed in the process. Empowering others to be their highest self in every part of life, including at work, is my life purpose.

The Urgency of Now (push back on racism and sexism in the workplace)

A leading non-profit research organization called Catalyst, working to advance women in business with offices in New York, San Jose, and Toronto, began releasing gender research results as early as 1997. These results furnished a rather dismal photograph of the career experience of women of color in management. Through their projects and advisory services, Catalyst has access to a wealth of data, which supports, on a larger scale, what African American and other women of color live on a daily basis. In 2002, only a small percentage of Fortune 500 corporate officers were women of color, (106 out of 10,092) (Catalyst, *2002 catalyst Census of Women Corporate Officers and Top Earners of the Fortune 500).* Fifteen years later, McKinsey & Company together with Leanin. Org conducted a study, *"Women in the Workplace 2017,"* publishing that while more companies are committing to gender equality, progress continues to be very slow, particularly regarding women of color.

While women remain underrepresented in corporate America at every conceivable level, women of color confront more obstacles, and a much rockier road to leadership. They are promoted more slowly and receive much less support from managers. In spite of their education and advanced degrees, they trail behind white men, men of color, and white women in all industries. They receive fewer promotions at entry-level employment and they have less opportunity to interact with senior-level management. This data affirms the challenges for women of color within organizations. Their success is oppressed from the very beginning of their professional career.

This book is a prescription for how women of color should navigate and push back on the traditional notion of maintaining the status quo in the workplace. Women of color everywhere can articulate with clarity the environmental factors and social risks that impede the growth, wellness, and prosperity across a multitude of industry, disciplines, and issues. They have the competence and courage to address and solve some of the most protracted issues and dilemmas of our time with grace and a sense of urgency. Those organizations who included women of color in the decision making and problem-solving process have outperformed their non-inclusive peer group. I recommend that you to commit to the principles set forth in *Twice as Good* as a method of resistance and empowerment.

Now Is Your Time

This is a time when others are beginning to recognize the gifts, talents, and abilities of women of color in society—specifically in the political realm. It's about time that our society is finally getting a clue on the capacity of women of color. Now is your time to get clear about what you want and get ready to take action.

Although it's an exciting time to be a woman of color in the work place, it is also a double-edged sword fraught with invisible impediments.

Tactfully handled situations bring great rewards, yet misaligned zeal may lead to curtailed career growth. It's been a slow yet steady process as companies and the work culture are learning that women of color matter as key drivers to organizational success. Your hard work combined with a willingness to challenge established status quos is threatening. Yet that combination of skill and integrity with an authentic zeal for doing what is needed and what is right is what organizations require to create a more equitable and inclusive society.

Women of color have always and will continue to be disrupters of the status quo through their leadership at work and in society.

My dissertation through Pepperdine's Graduate School of Education and Psychology focused on the leadership behaviors and practices of executive women of color in higher education. The single most important finding in the research study was the degree to which women of color challenged the decision-making processes in all areas more than their peer counterparts (white females). Another way of describing this is that women of color counteracted and questioned elements of organizations that were static and traditional. In doing so, they sought to create new forms of operational excellence that were more inclusive and mission-aligned. In my research, women of color pushed against the status quo in every single dimension of the work environment and when the data was distributed by race, Black women had the highest level of challenging social norms within organizations that were harmful to inclusion than other women of color.

The McKinsey/Leanin. Org study "Women in the Workplace 2017" collected data from 222 companies with collectively more than 12 million employees combined with a survey of over 70,000 employees. They found that while one in five of C-suite leaders is a woman, only one in thirty is a woman of color, and yet these same women of color, who have fewer opportunities for advancement, are more entrepreneurial. They are more likely to say that they will start their own businesses if they leave their actual job. We see more Latinas becoming entrepreneurs and business owners than any single other demographic in California and throughout key parts of the United States.

This entrepreneurial spirit is what defines corporate America and its global success, and you are a large part of it. A year later, their 2018 survey showed a continuation of this trend. They surveyed 279 companies with over 13 million employees. They interviewed 64,000 workers and the results were similar to the year before. The risk and reality is that progress is happening but so slowly that it may not be perceived to matter as it should.

You know how to lead. It's already within you. You will challenge status quos for good and when no one else has the courage and strength to do it. This leadership framework will focus your energies and efforts for success.

Finally, I hope to connect and share my experience and research from the thousands of individuals I have personally worked to the thousands of others who will never walk into my office, hear me give a speech, or take a graduate course with me. Together, we can make meaningful change for women of color who are primed and ready to assume greater professional roles right where they are.

Some of you will be ready to go the next level now and need support. There is a direct line between my story of leadership and power and your story of leadership and power. My hope is to position and inspire you to get where you are meant to be soon.

Chapter 1

Race and Gender as Formation

"America is composed of all kinds of people—part of the difficulty in our nation today is due to the fact that we are not utilizing the abilities and the talents of other brown and black peoples and females that have something to bring to the creativity and the rejuvenation and the revitalization of this country."
– Shirley Chisholm

I lost my mother over the time of writing this book and before it was complete.

She was born in rural Central Arkansas during the Jim Crow segregation in 1934. I am learning more about her early life and where she lived. She grew up in a loving black home and black community and excelled in school. Her father was a Baptist minister. Her mother grew beautiful vegetables. She ran track in high school and was known for being fast. Outside of the state-sanctioned terrorism of Jim Crow which excluded African Americans from fully participating in daily activities and prohibited them from engaging as full citizens in society, her family, church, and community life were great as it was all Black.

However, she also experienced and endured through what we know today as one of the worst periods of American public policy accompanied by public acceptance and opinion that treated African Americans without regard, respect, or dignity as human beings.

This period post-Reconstruction was a political and economic assault and attempt to diminish the collective imagination and ingenuity of a specific population of people in the United States. There was a systemic and structured endeavor to limit and destroy the capacity of African Americans to earn and gain a prosperous livelihood for their family coupled with a social, educational, and spiritual attempt to crush the spirit of a people and their pursuit of life, liberty, and happiness.

Remnants of this era continue today.

As they became adults and finished their education in segregated high schools, my mother and her siblings began to make their way into the world as young adults; migrants leaving their rural home seeking a better life in other parts of the country. Some of my uncles served in the military. Nearly all of my mother's brothers went north where a steady flow of Black migration had already begun toward the great industrial cities where good jobs were available for African Americans.

My mother and her sisters decided to go out West to California.

Her migration decision would change everything and set my life on an amazing trajectory as a native California kid, born and raised. Through an act of migration, my parents gave their children the most multicultural, pluralistic community experience imaginable. Everybody on the block and in the neighborhood, was an immigrant and came from someplace else. Most of my friends in the neighborhood were all first-generation Californians. I was immersed in a rich diversity of ethnicities and cultures in school and in the community where people had close ties to their cultural heritage. Multiple languages were spoken, diverse religions were observed and practiced, and ethnic foods and their markets abounded. To illustrate my upbringing, my Latinx friends' families were mostly from the central states of Mexico like Michoacán, my Filipino friends were nearly all first-generation Americans whose parents had migrated from the Philippines, the Italians and Irish had grandparents who migrated through Ellis Island before coming to the California Central Valley—many due to the pull of the agricultural region. My friends and their families who were Roman Catholics had a common language of Christianity that I understood and through which we bonded.

Most of the African American families like mine had ties to the southern states and nearly all of our parents were the first-generation cohort to reside in California. My black friends were mostly the children of the Great Migration as I was. We were the first group of California born children. Our Chinese neighbors came before most of the other ethnic communities of color and were a combination of recent immigrants and second or third generation Chinese Americans. All of my Japanese American school friends were the children of internment camp survivors. From a religious perspective, we were as diverse as can be. Most of the African Americans were Baptists like Dr. Martin Luther King, Jr. had been. The Germans and a few other Europeans were Protestants. The Greeks in the community went to a primarily Greek Orthodox church. And my Japanese and Chinese school friends grew up in Buddhist households. There was a community of Sikhs in town who I knew from school.

By 1976, I was introduced to my first cohort of Vietnamese, Laotian and Hmong classmates who immigrated to my community. Each year it seemed as though there were more refugee children arriving to our neighborhood and other neighborhoods from Southeast Asia. They would show up to class one day and be there with me and the school age youth. It would take years later for me to fully understand what they had recently experienced in their journey to sit next to me in the classrooms. The dangerous, dark open waters of their exits, leaving all that they knew behind as they fled often in the middle of the night as political and social refugees and freedom seekers, to come to the United States for a better life. Thousands would settle in my hometown. Most Southeast Asian immigrants were Buddhist as my Japanese friends were. Some were Christian. Eventually they would build their own temples, often in unincorporated areas in the outskirts of town.

We all went to school together. We all played sports together. We all hung out together. Without being aware of it at the time, I was learning about humanity through spending time playing with my old and new friends. Due to the steady flow of immigrant children who came to our community, I wondered why they left everything they knew behind and what it was like getting on a boat to travel and live where I lived. The only forms of transportation I knew of was the city bus, the school bus (for field trips), and my dad's old Ford truck and the new Chevy Impala.

It would be some years later when I made my first known Jewish friends in college. It happened in the dormitory, outside of the classroom learning environment where I was finally able to learn about the Jewish religion and their culture and traditions from peers who were actually Jewish—beyond what I thought I knew from Sunday School class at church.

Everyone had a culture, a language, traditions, and foods that gave them a sense of uniqueness, faith, and pride for a culturally-informed and culturally-grounded American identity. Personally, I had my Black American culture, my Black church, my Black family and all the magic that came with it.

My mother gave me the gift of living in cultural diversity with diverse people and their diverse experiences, no less the stories of people who were different than my own. Coupled with her own courageous migration experience, her siblings and the migration of my father, my sisters and I were fortunate to have early life experiences with race and gender and that introduced different people that were familial, normal, and beautiful.

The racial and gender socialization I experienced went far beyond the limited black and white binary and narrative that we often saw reflected in the media. Even more so, the perspective that the country was either black or white and that everything important was done or led by white people only, was presented to us as children through our curriculum books at school, but that was not a reality where I lived.

There was little, if no, mention of people of color in the school textbooks and for some reason it wasn't questioned—or at least I didn't know of anyone who questioned. And when African Americans or Native Americans, specifically, were mentioned, I didn't see the pride and vibrancy of the multicultural women and men in my community. Everything I learned about the actual achievement or contribution of Black people came from home or at church. In my community, Black people were makers and creative. We were singers and preachers. We danced, wrote, and invented music, and excelled at sports. We taught school, built houses, and worked for the post office. Black people were entrepreneurs and owned and operated businesses like automotive, beauty, and barber shops. We worked for the city government and the school district. We were hardworking, full of life, and talented.

I did not fully understand it at the time, yet our lived experiences as people of color in the neighborhood was not in line with what I saw about myself or others like me from the nightly news or television. What I knew came from direct encounters and experiences with mostly other people of color from diverse parts of the world. We assembled together through a common zip code. We shared essential establishments like the fish and meat market, the hardware and department store, schools, a park, and a library.

Where my mother chose to raise her children informed and impacted everything I know about gender, race, and class in America even through today. The brilliant part of all of this is that while I was immersed in a deeply multicultural, multi-lingual, and intra-faith living and learning environment, she also provided me access to learn my identity and what Blackness meant. My mother was under no false pretense regarding how the country disregards the gifts and talents of African Americans.

Having experienced segregation firsthand, she knew what oppression felt like beyond anything a college textbook or university lecture could communicate or fully capture. She knew about the concept of positionality as a lived experience, knowing full well the places she was invited and the places she could not go when desired.

She made sure we had a strong foundation in our faith, our history, and our cultural identity through raising me within the Black community and the Black Church.

Through my Black identity I know *Twice as Good* as an inspiration to push beyond the limited goals society had for me; a strategy and perhaps prescription Black parents gave their children for living and potentially thriving in America.

This notion of being excellent was what was available to her and other Black parents in preparing their children for an uneven and unfair playing field. "You're going to have to work twice as hard, and be twice as good in everything, baby," she would remind me. "And they're not going to give you any breaks, especially if they see you are good."

Now exactly who the "they" were that she spoke of, and how I would try to figure out what she really meant in her wisdom and advice would take years to decode and understand.

Disrupting "Twice as Good"

In college, the humanities curriculum gave me a language to further make sense of what was going on with the experiences of women and people of color. Through history, sociology, and literature, I was able to better articulate why I had always felt there was something wrong with having to work harder than everyone else.

I could finally put my finger on what really bothered me. I learned that racism and sexism were not only realities that occur on the individual level, from one person to another, but were part of an intentional social and economic structure that determined how and where people start in life. Even how fast and how far they progress was informed by structural inequity and supported by public policy and laws.

The racism and sexism we experience today was constructed by certain individuals and could have been avoided. What an epiphany that was for me as a young person.

I realized how much of my experience was engineered by people. By leaders appointed to improve society. The interests of groups of businessmen, politicians, and law makers—individuals and groups homogenous and similar to one another. Personal economic interests, mainly on the basis of sustaining class through capital, had a profound impact in creating the modern-day disparities we recognize along race, gender, and class. I sensed that individual effort alone could never ameliorate the engineered reality of structural inequity.

This is why "You're going to have to be twice as good and work twice as hard" had become my mantra. Being both black and female in the United States would have some challenging days ahead. Ok, I had been prepared for this by the loving adults in my life. They had warned me in advance. They believed my best defense against racism was an offense of personal excellence. That was my play. It was on me to fix things by being and doing better against the odds.

Revelation and Resistance

I came to the revelation that the history of Black and other people of color revealed an attempt and successful effort to systemically prioritize and protect the interest of an elite class of males and their families. The comfort and prosperity of a class of white people came at the expense of people of color and other marginalized groups. This was normal and practiced on a daily basis.

As time progressed, to prioritize and protect those interests would mean to attempt to diminish the fullness of Black joy and Black prosperity. Even more so, white supremacy was much more than outrageous clans of individuals who were outliers in society lurking in wait to harm people of color as we were taught in school. White supremacy existed to prioritize the comfort and prosperity of white people at the expense of all people of color and was as American as apple pie. White supremacy was not a fringe group of bad individuals, yet rather an ideology of supremacy that provided for and allowed unearned advantage in all areas of society to persist for some without them even being aware of their participation and enjoyment in it.

Leadership behavior in the workforce, then, was an evolved expression of white supremacist thinking in organizations. A byproduct of white supremacy that had become perfected and disguised as management practice in the American workplace. That explained to me why expressions of misogyny and racism were actually normal, expected behaviors considering who led organizations. It would take social justice movements including labor rights, civil rights, women's rights through court battles with enacted legislation to begin to course correct the centuries of repression and exclusion.

Twice as Good instructed me to look at others as the measure of what success looks like—others who were white and mostly male as the standard of how successful is behaviorally coded, who decides, and how success is determined.

My graduate level social justice education provided social and economic analysis and applied research skills to deconstruct how problematic and damaging Twice as Good is for Black and brown children. The Twice as Good standard left large segments of children behind as they started life with disparities in outcomes and this would continue through their childhood into adulthood. They had invisible yet real barriers in their lives. Every important facet of American life had life-altering remnants for children in education, healthcare, and socioeconomic outcomes. Was this their fault? And was it all on them to overcome?

I maintained an optimism in spite of this that had come from my family and community. All I knew for sure was that an individual Black girl had to keep moving and stepping forward to get things done for herself. I finally understood why this African American proverb (Twice as Good) never felt 100% right to me, even while I was doing it.

As an educator, I would wonder what would happen if organizations, businesses, and institutions used their platforms to do something about inequality for women and people of color. Could corporate values of diversity and inclusion permeate society beyond the walls of a major organization? Would institution leaders and trustees embrace their role to influence the lives of people like me? Does any major institution or corporate entity exist that truly cares about the freedom and liberty of women of color?

Over time, I would discover how the workplace became an active environment for *Twice as Good* to thrive and that it was a problematic reality. Twice as Good is a preemptive gesture or defense, if you will, to enacted organizational expression to unconsciously and consciously diminish (and at times destruct) the beauty and possibility of what it means to be a woman of color in the workplace. I knew this could not continue to be the only means available people of color for their success. I chose to persist, with what I knew from my upbringing and experiences, in spite of the injustice.

Movement and Migration

My mother and her siblings were part of what is called the Great Migration where six million African Americans exited the southern region of the country, becoming the largest movement of migrants known in the world. These migrants were social and political refugees who needed to relocate to find freedom within their own country.

I come from a legacy of freedom seekers and dream makers. I believe that women of color are dreamers and seekers, seeking individual freedom and freedom for others. That's an ultimate goal I see in the millennial women of color I encounter each day. I particularly love teaching and working with these younger women who teach me about leadership. They are open about their shared pain, shared pleasure, shared frustration, and shared righteous anger as they plan to live their life out more fully and in a beautifully grand and integrated manner.

To accompany someone in their journey and to guide steps along the way is a privilege and responsibility. I will share the insights I have learned plus the lessons others have taught me. Through personal narrative, I will guide the reader on how to challenge the process and how to push against the status quo of tradition that creates an invisible yet real wall of resistance to your full inclusion in the workplace. I share stories of childhood formation that inform and shape how I show up as an executive woman of color and what that means or looks like on a daily basis. And how my work as an executive leader and professor focuses on the intersectionality of social identities and how gender and race play roles today in shaping the American workplace.

Storytelling as leadership development. This is how we leverage cultural wisdom not found in business schools and we create new dimensions on how to become and how to engage the difficult and troubled waters of race and gender. Through the lens of the lived experiences of women of color, we learn what it means to be powerful.

You are reading this book at the right moment in your life and in the right time in history. Women of color are being called to their rightful place of leadership in all areas of our social order. The socio-political-economic wind is shifting and voices of reason, strength, and courage are called to their vocation and required for change. We need leaders who have a commitment to diversity in all its' forms, equity, and equality. We need leaders who will focus on results that are fair and economically equitable.

We need leaders who can take up the mantle with a focus on the inclusivity of everyone. We need leaders who are equity-minded in their approach that builds community across difference. We need leaders who tell the truth. We need leaders who can talk about race. We need leaders who can prioritize the stories and experiences of communities who have been left behind. We need leaders who come from marginalized and vulnerable backgrounds.

You are that leader. Here is some insight about why you should be taken seriously at work on your own terms and how this book can assist you in that effort:

You legitimize your organization's rhetoric around diversity and inclusion. Whatever they say about their commitment to ideals of social responsibility, diversity, etc., it's your presence, participation and contribution that matters at the end of the day. Their corporate commitment to doing good for humanity hinges on how well you are able to contribute your genius and competence in a full and whole manner. Your company wears the mantle of diversity integration thanks to your presence and your talent. But companies must go further in their commitment to gender and ethnic diversity. You are not present in order to guarantee numbers and percentages for reporting purposes.

You are there because of your talent, excellence, and commitment. You bring success and validity to corporate and non-profit America. Their authentic business and profit growth over time depends on your level of representation, enacted voice, and upward mobility.

Excellence through diversity brings better results, greater rewards. If corporate America is to continue to maintain its economic preeminence globally, it must tap the enormous talent pool available, available through women of color in leadership. Criteria for hiring and promotion based on inclusivity must be established and implemented. It is not enough to be invited to the table if you are not allowed to cook up and partake of the meal.

You are ready more than you may know. This is your call to action.

Reflection:

Think of your earliest memories of becoming aware of gender and race. What did you learn about gender and what did you learn about race? How did you learn this and whom did you learn from? What well-intended message may have become harmful to you along the way? What actions can you take today to disrupt that messaging?

Chapter 2

Change the Narrative
on What's Possible

My Story, Part 1

I was a twenty-nine-year-old professional when I first become a dean at a California public university. I had returned from my first maternity leave where I took a mere seven weeks off. Within two months of my return, I interviewed and was offered the role of Assistant Dean of Students. I was ecstatic and I was so proud. My life then was a flurry of schedules and to-do lists.

I was in San Diego County with a new born and lacked familial support as my family was concentrated in Northern California. I was nursing my new baby girl; pumping and storing milk for her during the workday. Attempting to create as many opportunities for bonding experiences, I found a family daycare nearby the university campus. Although it was less than five miles away, with getting out of the office on time and moving through traffic, it was a frustrating experience trying to see my daughter during lunch breaks. The work itself at the university was rewarding and stimulating. Integrating my life as a young mother and young professional was difficult yet I was grateful for my employer and work life. Most of the time my life felt clumsy.

I was new at my first major job and I had so much to learn. I felt a pull between getting to my baby daughter during the day and the need to demonstrate a commitment to the work as a professional in an important organizational role.

It was the mid-1990s and my promotion was a big deal. African American women were grossly underrepresented in the field of university administration. I wanted to take the extra steps to be the best assistant dean I needed to be. I was the chief conduct officer so all violations of the university student code of conduct were handled in my office, personally by me.

Academic dishonesty such as cases of severe plagiarism landed on my desk. Poor behavior like calling the professor or classmate a derogative term landed on my desk. Getting caught smoking pot on campus landed on my desk. There was a council of faculty and staff that reviewed the academic integrity cases. There was another council to look at the non-academic behavioral issues. I led both groups and had to be fair and impartial in my investigative process and ensure that students' rights, privileges, and responsibilities were upheld to the university's standard, yet balanced to provide a teachable and developmental moment for the involved student.

I had anxiety about possibly getting the wrong outcome on a case. I was concerned about being taken seriously, especially when I dealt with students who were older than myself. I was also scared a lot in those early days of my career. Actually, I was scared most of the time.

I was scared that my baby would fall in love with her caregivers more than with me because of the time I spent away from her. I was scared that my boss would think I wasn't good enough and that she may had made a mistake in promoting me. I was scared that I might mess things up with just one scheduling mishap in my bumbling, busy life as a new mother and working professional.

I was scared and conflicted nearly all the time in those very early professional years; I had a bad case of impostor syndrome that was playing out in full effect. Yet this was the beginning of my future as an executive woman of color. I was filled with internal dissonance and I was just getting started. Who was I to be young, female, and Black and a dean at a state university?

My Story, Part 2

When the opportunity came across my desk to live and work in Los Angeles and the prospect to become a dean of student affairs with a broad-based portfolio of responsibility, I went for it. I was ready for a change and new challenge and felt like a fresh start in a different city would be good for me. I had given birth to a second baby girl and their father and I were separated. Both of my young daughters came to work with me now as the university's early learning center opened for preschool age children. The employer-sponsored learning center may have saved my sanity and health. It was a gift from God and a relief that only a single working mother can truly understand.

It is almost too difficult to articulate in words what that early learning center meant to me as a young professional with a demanding job. A good childcare or early learning center was the most important resource in my life. At times, it felt more important than the job itself.

I was getting better at being a dean and regularly took work home. Don't ask me how I managed to work all day and then take care of two beautiful little toddler, pre-K girls. I just did it. Too much from that time is a blur because of the busyness of the days. There was a storm building inside of me and it was gathering wind and sometimes pressure. Yet, I continued to do it all and worked twice as hard as always and kept the pace for what I needed to be successful.

My daughters' father and I had been separated and the final date for the divorce had come. That dean of student affairs job announcement forwarded by a friend was timely. I interviewed in Los Angeles. I got the job. This was my daughters' first move from the place they were born. As much as I had enjoyed San Diego, I was ready to leave.

We spent the next eight years in Los Angeles and it was a time of significant opportunity and personal growth. I loved West Los Angeles. We were situated in Marina del Rey and Playa Vista and we enjoyed hanging out in Santa Monica and mid-Wilshire on the weekends. Free quality educational resources abounded for my daughters to get involved and engaged in the community; and I was resourceful as a working single parent.

The children's art program at the Los Angeles County Art Museum (LACMA) was a fantastic institution as the girls participated in their children's community program and painted and made art in a wonderful studio on Saturdays at no cost. Culver City became a favorite destination as the girls started growing up in Los Angeles and would meet up with their friends to watch movies. There was the $2 matinee on Saturdays in Downtown Culver City that was a hit with children and families and a dependable outing as the finances were tight. As I always looked out for the quality of their education, we moved to Culver City for my daughters to attend middle school in a highly rated public school district.

I was surrounded by art, design, and fashion as the dean at one of the finest art colleges in the country. The environment was stimulating for me and invited my own creativity to emerge and flow. Being in the midst of artists and designers became my life as we lived so close to the campus that I would pop in to my office any given weekend with my daughters in tow. I would check on work items or even better, to just see what my students were up to as they worked in their school-sponsored studios all of the time.

As a working professional with children, I was busy and I stayed distracted. The Twice as Good narrative would continue as I worked as hard as I could to be as good as possible in each area of life.

I was having lunch with a friend who I truly looked forward to being with any time I could see her. She was one of sharpest and most authentic women I had met in Los Angeles. She, too, worked in higher education and was well regarded in the field and within her college community. During one of our conversations, being twice as good emerged as a theme that I did not expect at that time and would determine what would happen next in my life. My friend had also become a mentor in the field and a role model. She was married to a well-known and recognizable actor and had an admirable career and life. They traveled to great locations and had a lovely home in Los Angeles. She was down-to-earth, accessible, and completely unpretentious about it all. She had founded and led an annual hike for women of color—an invitation-only group of sisters in a carefully curated and exploratory mountain range and hiking experience. I think I admired her so much because she saw me. She invited me in to her life. Her life was fabulous in my eyes. I wanted to emulate her. I wanted to learn from her. She wore great shoes. She had earned a doctorate.

She didn't say the exact words, yet it was an advisement I had heard before. "They aren't going to take you serious, Mary, without that doctoral degree." I listened carefully as she spoke to me directly. I knew exactly what she meant by "they." I had heard the proverbial term of "they" from my childhood. The tone of her voice and the commentary she made to me felt familiar, even familial. She was communicating truth to me out of love. The same way I had heard it from a handful of other women of color, like my mother, along the way.

I wasn't upset when she told me this, yet I wanted to come up with reasons about how I would be able to continue on my trajectory based upon a few other people I had met in the field. Although I was able to cite examples of other women in higher education positions with a master's degree who were successful vice presidents, she gave me the look. The look that only an experienced woman of color gives a less experienced woman of color. My friend and mentor, who is African American, reminded me that in all my examples they were white and I was not. She had already worked in higher education for at least thirty years when we met.

She was a seasoned woman of color in a field with only a few black women. She worked twice as hard to get there. She passed on her hard-earned wisdom to me out of love and duty.

I knew then what needed to be done.

Within twelve months of that conversation, I was enrolled in a doctoral program. I decided on Pepperdine as the university had a campus in Culver City and their Graduate School of Psychology and Education was housed there. The cohort program I wanted to attend met nearby. My home was close. My work was close. My daughters' school was nearby. It could not have been a more perfect geographical situation and I felt that it was meant to be.

Yet, I was about to get even more busy. My girls were school age. I worked full time. And I was a single working parent starting a full-time doctoral program of study.

It would seem that I was a victim to the twice as good narrative again; because I was.

I successfully completed my coursework and dissertation in five years. I didn't finish on-time which would have been four years, yet I was not in the back end of the cluster trailing behind. This was remarkable considering the complexity of my life compared with classmates without children and less demanding work schedules. Basically, my track record for the degree completion was outstanding considering what was on my plate. I may not have been twice as good in the program, per se, yet I was moving through barriers and checking off goals along the way at a pace that others around me weren't doing. Beyond attaining a terminal degree in my field, I completed a research study on a topic that I cared about. Women of color in leadership and understanding what happens with them was important and relevant for me because it was my personal narrative. This doctoral program work product would inform my future trajectory in ways that I could never imagine as a future diversity and inclusion leader and became central and integrated into every aspect of my identity and work.

My time in Los Angeles was nearing its end as an opportunity in San Francisco was presented to me. I was ready to take a leap of faith again. A new job and new city. I had finished what I had started at Pepperdine. Those eight years in Los Angeles had been important to get to the next level. I had been a successful dean at a great college and I had earned a doctorate degree while building my career. As a working mother, my confidence seemed to be through the roof especially post-divorce as I knew that I was strong and could do anything I set my mind to; even on my own.

I was on top of the world and felt like I could accomplish any goal I set. To be twice as good, you must work twice as hard. Not only did I know how to be twice as good, I was excelling at doing so. Although I still did not like the need to work so hard to secure a future for myself and my daughters, I felt I was making significant progress and all was under control.

In time, I would learn that it all came at a price. I suppressed the introspection and reflection work that was necessary and needed to be a whole person; a function that comes from a place of truth and authenticity. So far, I had proved I could set goals and meet them. And had proved that I was organized enough and determined enough. I knew how to schedule my time to get things done. I had proved that I could handle the pressure and wouldn't cave or concede during challenges. I placed the bet on myself and I was winning.

However, I missed making investments in relationships, including the relationship with myself. The kind of personal relationship that was caring and true. The kind of self-relationship that would help me become whole in my relationships with others. I held on to hurts from my past and kept them hidden. I tucked them away as I embraced and fulfilled more complex professional opportunities.

I was aware my daughters missed their mom while I was busy going after my schooling and career, yet they were growing up with adventure and independence as a central theme of their lives. I justified being busy as I gave them opportunity to have other experiences with other diverse families and individuals—often fabulous and smart young college students who were their babysitters, who probably taught my daughters things a bit too early. And wonderful family friends who took my girls in just like one of their own. They had role models from being with other mothers and fathers. They became comfortable being with people. My daughters were becoming strong on their own. I had transferred to them what I learned and had been modeled for me.

My daughters probably grew up fast with a professional working mother. We spent quality mom and daughter time together for sure. At times, there were activities in their schooling that I missed. I didn't make it for the classroom parties or most of the parental involvements. Yet if they were speaking or performing, I never missed that. As young adults now, they recall that time as wonderful and they think I was a great mom and role model of Black womanhood. Still, I ponder on what I could have done better.

I moved to San Francisco and carried on as I had before. It took another six years before I began to seriously do the interior work to peel back the effects of what I call a cumulative assault on being black and female. I had to find ways to heal. If the San Diego years were foundational, the Los Angeles years developmental, then, if I were to become my true and highest self, the San Francisco years were going to have to be transformational.

My professional identity and work is where I have given so much of myself and the best place for me to begin this internal work. It was in this discovery process that being twice as good was now a trigger reminding me of all the attempts I've made to close my own achievement gap in society and how hard I'd work against ensuring strong outcomes for myself.

Deep down I had become weary and frustrated with the Twice as Good notion because it had been unfair, unjust, and had come at a personal cost. I had work to do. And during my years in San Francisco I would launch deep within the interior of life to better understand who I had become and who do I need to be. The eventual healing would come.

My Story, Part 3

Returning to Northern California was good for my soul. Coming to San Francisco to live and work afforded me the opportunity to connect with family more often. Being close to home was healing and necessary after being away from my Northern California home base for eighteen years. My leadership opportunities and professional reputation expanded in San Francisco during this time. I arrived as a dean and senior student affairs executive and was appointed the inaugural chief diversity officer at a major urban university. My work was remarkably meaningful and challenging at the same time.

My life was evolving and there was a calling for wellness in every aspect of the word. I engaged in retreat experiences, took up yoga, and read a lot of books and immersed myself in topics on integrating wholeness and healing as principles for living a complete spiritual life. I met and married a life partner during this time who provided the kind of love and support I needed. I could do my own internal work and be in a relationship. Plus, I had a lot of growth and development of my own to do in the area of companionship and learning how to be in a relationship with a partner was important work to do.

On a day-to-day basis, I enjoy time alone to think, create, ponder, and enjoy nature and the miracles we see in the world. I began to seek and look for the kind of people who had a generous spirit and whose energy connects with my own. I was joyful being in the presence of kindred spirits.

On the professional side, I was becoming masterful as a leader in the diversity, equity and inclusion space and grew as a leader recognizing and understanding institutionalized forms of racism and sexism and their impact on women of color in the academy. My work gave me a platform to examine and discuss how gender inequity had become a normalized and coded way of doing business as usual. I noted how women and people of color were made invisible in a manner that was unconscious to the offender, the institution itself, and how racial and gender injustices might even fool some people of color while they were being impacted in covert and seemingly innocuous ways.

I carefully studied the literature on how oppression worked within organizations and the best strategies deployed to keep it in place. I noted how women of color always were the ones who found themselves at the hands of institutional racism and gender inequity in this pattern of intersectional phenomena. I could even predict where organizational problems might emerge before an issue became apparent or known. I became extra attentive to the lived experiences and conditions of all persons on campus who were from any marginalized background or community, and was able to relate their experiences to my own experience and identity. More importantly, was to connect the research to lived experiences of women of color in the workplace. I found a passion as a diversity, equity and inclusion leader.

Success in Supporting Women of Color

I have guided women through unseen and often unknown barriers in the workforce that exist. Unfortunately, there isn't a roadmap on how to navigate these barriers, although testimony and narratives offer insight. They are often invisible and women of color need to prepare for them even when they are not easily identifiable.

Reflection:

"If you desire the highest appointment, work for and attain a doctoral degree." In my heart, I knew my colleague was telling me the truth. In this case, if you are an educational administrator or want to be one, a doctoral degree is a "must" as it gives you extensive training and experience to become an effective leader. For women of color in any field, the bar is set high.

What advisement have you been given or taken that was not required or expected in the same way with your peers? Describe a time when you could have been extended the benefit of the doubt yet understood that was not an option. To what extent, if any, was your gender and race a conscious factor in your effort to "qualify" and essentially be twice as good?

Chapter 3

Get Ready to Make Things Better

"My mother was a dominant force in our family. And that was great for me as a young woman, because I never saw that women had to be dominated by men."
— Dolores Huerta

Intergenerational Perspectives

In my research, I spent hours in conversations with women of color across generations and experiences. Today, I am the parent of two millennial women of color, both of whom are at the early stage of their career life and were perfectly conversant on the topic of being taken seriously as young women of color at work. My daughters are grounded in their identities and without the approval of the dominant culture.

I learn from the students I teach and the leaders I coach. What I learn I test in the classroom as part of the curriculum with my graduate business and education students, most of whom are professionals in the workplace. The women of color I mentor are critical to me as my work reflects their lived experiences. My work also reflects the experiences of retired executive women of color who I've included in interviews and coaching sessions. Veteran executive women of color represent the highest expression of what it means to step in to your power as they have demonstrated how to remain true to themselves despite changes in the workforce.

We stand on their shoulders as pathway-makers, blazing ahead. Veteran women of color worked against the restraints and limitations of racism and sexism long before many of us were born. There was much difficulty placed before them and put upon them. Nonetheless, their professionalism, grace, and resilience would result in realizing illustrious careers in business, law, government, education, healthcare, and array of other fields.

Passing on the equality baton is a theme for experienced women of color with younger women. There are lessons I learned from entering the professional workforce in the late 80s and early 90s with regard to how gender and race played out which can inform how differently gender equity plays out today for my daughters and my students. Some things stay the same and familiar across generations. I have my own veteran experience to inform the body of knowledge.

Post-Racial Ideation

Experienced women of color recall a period of time when organizations would unknowingly practice racism and gender inequity while at the same time promoting corporate-wide diversity initiatives. This was particularly the case after 2008 when Barack Obama was elected president. Let me explain.

Veteran diversity colleagues recall how peers held desperately to the notion that racism was a remnant of the past and insisted that diversity initiatives should focus on the celebration of diversity and the beauty of our uniqueness as individuals. The messaging was that diversity was celebratory in organizations. The work environment wasn't ready to hear that beyond overt and egregious displays of discrimination that, all in all, experiences among co-workers was generally fair and equal. Microaggression behavior, the everyday slights that accumulate over time, was deemed as communication misunderstandings between individuals. Perhaps persons of color may be overreacting in a sensitive manner because "racism is dead." Intention versus impact was the conceptual frame often referred to that would weigh in favor toward the innocence factor; and the not aware white offender.

I have found it interesting over the years how women of color rarely are afforded the benefit of innocence and are expected to educate others on their lack of awareness.

Diversity was approached from the individual's perspective, not the organizational perspective. While people of color were being promoted and moving up the organizational ladder in corporate environments, there was also a sort of hyper "pull-yourself-up-by-your-bootstraps" scenario that everyone now had an equal chance to fully participate in the new diversity and inclusion paradigm.

Minority models of success were made prominent in corporate collateral and faces of diverse leadership were featured in videos and brochures. It was common to find profiles of success with a lovely woman or man of color personifying and signaling that anyone could now make it.

In keeping with this post-racial ideation, the voices of women of color and their experiences were effectively further diminished. Now, organizations armed themselves with the idea that if black or brown women were not able to equally and fully participate in the life of the organization then their condition must be a byproduct of something outside of the organization or otherwise self-caused. Most likely she needed to do something different; something more for her own career success. She would need to change her hair to comport to industry standard. Or modify the sound of her voice for a more appropriate tone with discomforted co-workers. Or she needed additional leadership training and workshops on how to be a leader to better work with others. The problem could not possibly exist within the organization itself.

The notion that racism was alive and well within our organizations was disbelieved by large portions of the American workforce (not including underrepresented minorities).

Prior to the last few years, any mention of racism as an on-going experience for people of color in society or at work would have been met with a post-racial response that would look and feel like a rebuke by white people. They were subtly appalled at the suggestion of a less than optimistic view of racial and gender progress made. It took a series of sobering events to finally convince smart colleagues that race relations and gender equity are significant problems in society and at work. Thus, the emergence of social movements to help us acknowledge long-standing racial and gender injustices to name the issues and start to build consciousness—#BlackLivesMatter, #MeToo, #TimesUp.

People of color knew the truth. Women of color chose to manage themselves and their own needs and issues within the company and doing so among less informed colleagues. They learned to decide if and when it was required to say something, and if so, what approach might be taken to educate colleagues on how racism and misogyny in the workplace exist. Just how high were the stakes in any given situation? And what am I willing to give up, lose, or in a very rare instance, gain, for speaking up about this?

That was always the questions every woman of color leader would ask herself before she could engage and take on an important issue or possible crisis. If they were exhausted by it all or just didn't want to be the one to teach on that given day, women of color learned how to ignore statements that demonstrate how far colleagues had to grow and learn about the realities of microaggressions, racialized slights, and other forms of aggressive and passive behaviors at work.

It can still be challenging for groups of well-intentioned colleagues within an organization to move beyond the standard narrative that seeks to place blame on the single individual for a racist or misogynistic act. It's easier to operate within the diversity and inclusion space when you can name and blame a single person or a subset of persons who seem to always require further professional development. Yet those of us who have done this work know that is a false narrative. The whole body of organizations, people at all levels, with all kinds of jobs and backgrounds, need to learn how to do better in their equity and inclusion work.

Talking to others about what racism and sexism is and how it works in society and how it shows up at work is an emotional labor of love that takes significant energy and time. From the perspective of persons of color at work, that energy and time can be better used for the progress and prosperity of Black and brown folks, as opposed to perpetually having to set aside time to explain the pervasiveness of whiteness in our society.

What I know for sure is that well-meaning white colleagues who held on to a colorblind and gender equality ideology as the gold standard for how to engage diversity in the workplace needed help when they were confronted by evidence that racism is rampant and never ceased to stop. They were wrong all along. The society was wrong in leading people to believe that racism and gender inequity was a thing of the past. And unfortunately, women of color took on the emotional labor of explaining the truth.

The work ahead requires a tremendous effort in inter-group dialogue that women of color are well equipped to guide and lead with others.

And there are women of color, particularly among millennial women, who could and will choose not to that work for others.

Diversity and Technology

As I'm situated in San Francisco, I stay abreast of what's happening with the diversity statistics in well-known companies and brands. Women of color in technology is an area to pay close attention to. I am not astounded at the gender and racial imbalance in technology as some of the seemingly most progressive organizations in the country and world.

Technology organizations are young and have the chance to get things right early on. We see strong inclusion statements and rhetoric about diversity that do not match up to the organization's inclusivity reality. As an educator and leader in the diversity and inclusion field, I observe industries that are emergent and their leadership's response and approach to the awareness gap for diversity and inclusion in their organization.

Organizations on the whole lack accountable metrics for determining how effective diversity and inclusion efforts work. Part of the problem is that decision makers themselves have too few encounters with the inclusion and equity issues they seek to address. If you're not a woman of color and you are a CEO, how do you understand the complexity of gender and race in your organization and how that shows up in the experiences of employees? How do you improve your outcomes for this population? If you are a C-suite level leader and grew up in a homogenized environment and your first interaction with historically based inequity was maybe in college, how do you learn what it means to be vulnerable and marginalized in society and at work? Where does social justice empathy and training occur for corporate directors and their CEOs? There is not a diversity training or program that will provide a chief executive officer and their reports the diversity intelligence that comes only through lived experience and personal encounter with others who are different.

A sign, not the only one, that a technology company is serious about their diversity commitment is whether or not they have a woman of color in at least one or more of the following executive roles: Chair of the Board, Chief Executive Officer, Chief Operating Officer, Chief Financial Officer, Chief Technology Officer, Chief Marketing Officer, Chief Diversity Officer, Chief Innovation Officer and General Counsel. If there is not a woman of color sitting at the leadership table at the highest level of the organization with one of these roles or titles (or other similar senior titles) at your organization, regardless of industry, then the organization is bluffing everyone, including themselves, about their commitment to diversity and inclusivity.

Diversity is realized with having diversity. You don't talk about it. You just do it. As a chief diversity officer, I find this work of commitment to equity and inclusion is complex at times yet much simpler than people make it out to be. Corporate boards should require their executive leaders be diverse. Without setting the expectation for inclusivity in gender and race, there is little value to change the DNA of the organization. How might technology companies do business differently if women of color occupied key leadership roles? What better message to communicate that equity and inclusivity matters?

Out of all the industry that exists, technology companies may still have a shot to course correct with bold and disruptive leadership among a few influential allies that feature the leadership of women of color. Of course, all of this begins when the actual composition of the board itself is diverse enough. Without diversity among the members of the board, there is no credibility to hold the management accountable for anything related to diversity and inclusion, and all rhetoric about their commitment to diversity and inclusion rings hollow.

Thus, the occasional woman of color C-suite level executive who is hired and who represents the diversity and inclusion statement and espoused values can find herself as a corporate unicorn, operating under an extreme Twice as Good pressure cooker.

Representation matters and begins at the board level and should be reflected in executive senior leadership. Women of color are well equipped yet need people who understand their worth and will invest in their leadership.

Today marks a unique time in the nation for women of color. The world is open to ideas of how to shift the paradigm on gender and racial inequity. Although women of color have been leading from behind for decades and centuries, now is the time for them to take the helm of leadership. Now is your time to build upon the leadership of the #BlackLivesMatter movement and the energy of the #MeToo and #TimesUp movements to examine issues from a gender and racialized lens. Now is the time to follow the leadership of the women of color who made the most diverse, democratically-elected Congress in the history of the nation.

The circumstances of the world of work are inviting you to have an encounter with yourself and others as a leader that is deeply personal and actionable. There is a spiritual dimension to women of color in leadership. You must engage with the wisdom and knowledge already within in you about new ways of being, broader ways of knowing, and rich ways of understanding that are part of something that is more expansive than yourself yet requires your experience and knowledge to unfold and manifest.

I cannot describe what that means for you exactly, however, I know that persons who identify as African American, Latina/Latinx, Indigenous, Native American, Middle Eastern, Asian American, Pacific Islander, Queer, and members of the gender non-conforming family are being called to step into their power. Leadership is an act of collective solidarity and enacting faith, hope, and love as a calling for conscious change. The good news is that a few companies are moving beyond rhetoric and holding themselves accountable by hosting conversations and dialogues on gender and race and taking action.

This is why now is the precise moment for you to step into your power and be the transformative force for good at work. You want to get better leadership results and want to lead in a way that brings your whole identity to the workplace.

In the chapters ahead, you will hear personal stories of my own transformational process. Through sharing my stories, you can trust that I see you, understand you, and feel what you are going through. I have been an executive in my field for twenty-five years and know the complexity of navigating gender and race in the workplace. I have mentored and supported thousands of former students who are now successful professionals in the workforce living their dream. My hope is to make a difference and help propel your movement forward.

The 7 Principles to Leadership and Power

Step 1: Your Magic Is Your Identity. You will learn how identity is your secret power to push through any challenge at work.

Step 2: Finding Your Transformative Allies. You will learn how to find allies and why these individuals are important to your success. Authentic relationships with allies will lead you toward recognition and advancement.

Step 3: Self-Reflection as Your Power Tool. You will learn to utilize introspection and how self-reflection is important for your state of mind and being strategic.

Step 4: Use Your Voice; Tell Your Truth. You will learn the necessity of using your voice to speak up and how and when to tell your truth.

Step 5: Enacting Your Leadership. You will learn how to navigate and work through everyday leadership issues with confidence as a woman of color at work.

Step 6: Stepping into Your Power. You will learn how vulnerability is the boldness to unleash your distinct power.

Step 7: Crush Impostor Syndrome. You will learn how to identify and how to respond to impostor syndrome and the accompanying mental blocks.

Reflection:

In Preparation for the Journey Ahead

I want you to have a conversation with a veteran woman of color who has held a significant leadership role or continues to hold a senior leadership role in any field. Have a real conversation about what experiences she has had involving gender and race. Try to dive deep and listen carefully to understand and unpack her story. You should walk away with a greater awareness of intergenerational perspectives and insights on race and gender in the workplace.

Chapter 4

Identity Is Your
Magic in Leadership

Identity Matters

Bringing an identity-informed and culturally grounded identity through the door is a powerful way to approach and show up to work each day. Your identity, your gender, and your race, are a part of your secret power; it's your magic. Your identity makes you unique in what you do and informs how you lead. Identity matters. Identity awareness in organizations is a form of self-affirmation and institutional resistance when necessary. It's a good thing for women of color to resist homogeneity within organizations. Hoping to become like everyone else is self-destructive as identity is your advantage.

The good news is women of color are showing up fully and bringing their whole self at work. This occurs when there is a critical mass of people of color that engenders a sense of belonging and presence. You should seek out organizations and institutions with resource and affinity groups that support women of color. Or create spaces for identity to flourish by starting equity and inclusion groups right where you are. Women of color thrive when identity is affirmed as a space for organizational inclusion.

It's important to pay close attention to how people lead and how identity informs their leadership.

We are witnessing how women of color bring a renewed energy and a sense of hope and devotion to the issues and challenges of our time. Women of color lead collectively and with purpose, linking their identity and experiences to the persons and communities they seek to impact. Teaching leaders how to see others and how to listen for inclusivity is difficult to accomplish and takes commitment and investment. As most of the leaders running companies and organizations are white and male, an intensive deconstruction of white privilege would need to occur with a focus on their own identity awareness and the impact their identity has made in their businesses.

Women of color are paying attention and listening to the world. Whether this is an intuitive sense of awareness or a well-developed capacity to make judgment and business decisions that include ideas of equality and inclusion, they know business as usual is failing. Women of color recognize the moral imperative involved across a multitude of industry challenges and opportunities. They have a closer proximity to issues faced by communities being excluded, shut out, or left behind. They sense the urgency of looking at new solutions and know that what happens next will determine the future for generations to come.

You bring a leadership approach that focuses on service and love everywhere you go. You build a business culture that not only fulfills corporate goals but also seeks to create a caring work environment. By developing a management practice that pays attention to the people in the organization through feedback, you demonstrate how women of color lead by taking principled action to respond to their needs.

Intersectionality

Kimberle Crenshaw is one of my heroes. As a thought leader, legal scholar, and civil rights activist, I regularly assign her writings to my graduate business and education students. A founder in the field of critical race theory, Professor Crenshaw holds a double appointment at the UCLA School of Law and Columbia University. She is an authority on the interplay and the intersection of racism and sexism. Known for her work in intersectional feminism and intersectional theory she coined the term "intersectionality" as a frame to see the unique experiences of social identities, particularly among minorities, in relation to systems and structures of power, privilege, oppression and discrimination.

Professor Crenshaw's scholarship has been revolutionary for diversity leaders, practitioners, and equity educators such as myself. She offers a practical way for students and professionals to see complex social science phenomena with clarity through a new frame and way of seeing in what she calls "overlapping systems of oppression and discrimination that women of color are subject to due to their race, class and gender."

In my work with women of color, there has not been one consultation or dialogue series in which they were able to separate out their experience of being a woman from their experience with race. Gender and race are inseparable social identities for women of color in the workplace.

Professor Crenshaw gave us new language to understand and talk about race with intersectionality. To understand issues of gender for a woman of color, we must also evaluate their gender through the intersectional lens of race and other intersecting identities.

As identity is part of our leadership and power, intersectionality offers an analytic frame that not only validates the unique experience of women of color leaders, it helps us to understand the ways our leadership shows up in organizations and why we show up in the manner that we do. Professor Crenshaw discusses how you can only change the things that you can see. For women of color in leadership, you can only acknowledge the strength of your identity by seeing how you uniquely approach issues and challenges as an intersectional person and being. The reason why women of color are so uniquely positioned to step into their power is that they have intersectional experiences and perspectives to offer to organizations; perspectives that create new possibilities and disrupt the limitation of the leadership we see in the world.

Women of color see problems at the intersections. Women of color develop solutions at the intersections. Society requires leaders with intersectional identities, who have intersectional lived experiences, to see intersectionality in everyday issues, to offer fresh intersectional solutions.

Intersectionality as a framing tool is complex and practical at the same time. It makes common sense when applied to replace binary approaches. The intersectionality of women of color and what they bring to the table offers leaders and policy makers an opportunity to reimagine issues and what can be done.

Bring Your Whole Identity to Work

I recently did a coaching session with a leader and she shared with me how she felt at work. She went on to say, "There are a lot of people who will never understand me or know my experiences as a Cambodian American woman. I feel alone in the workplace. When I speak up and challenge anything I feel like I'm deemed a problem and like people want me to fall into my place. Things that people in my workplace would never acknowledge as being unfair." My response to her was to learn more. I wanted to guide her into a productive discovery process grounded in the power of her intersectional identity.

Does her experience sound familiar to you? She was frustrated and discouraged by the lack of multicultural awareness in her work environment and the profound normativity and casualness of it all.

I appreciated her openness first, to herself and then, to me. Being open to talking about racial inequity through personal experience is significant for women of color. This degree of self-awareness is necessary as she continues to embrace just how valuable her identity is in her specific work environment.

The work for her was to learn and decide how her identity benefits everything that matters and how she shows up. We worked the signature 7 principles on leadership and power outlined in Chapter 3. Her leadership development will depend on the degree to which she is able to become grounded in her unique, intersectional identity to make a difference now and move forward to the next opportunity.

Cultural Magic

There is no secret that companies, businesses, and institutions benefit greatly from diversity. Individuals from different backgrounds, practices, beliefs, experiences, and so on bring innovation, growth, understanding, and compassion to the work place. These differences are the biological building blocks for our present-day evolution; our magic. It's about individuals who possess a different style and approach who will propel their unique ideas forward. It is this cultural magic that will guide and create an inclusive society.

More importantly, it's about representation. Knowing your worth and the reason why you are there. The first thing for all women of color is representation. It's not just representation within your group but being represented in the larger community.

Reflection:
Reflection:

On Identity

How do you identify? Born and raised in Oakland, Atlanta, Brooklyn, Chicago, D.C., Seattle? Are you shaped by the culture of a specific community of color? Other communities of color? How might your identities create a powerful platform in everything you do? Your identity is your fundamental foundation. It is exactly what people perceive when they see or encounter you but will not tell you to your face. Your identity is the thing that separates your knowledge from others and is exactly what is needed in the workplace. Understanding the ways in which your identity is your secret power will be critical in your transformation as a powerful leader.

I'm encouraging you to be more conscious than you have been in the past about who you are and what it means for you to be a Latina, to be Asian, to be multi-racial, to be gender fluid, and so on.

In a male dominated world and white male dominated society, people of color and women of color are often misunderstood. Given this reality, you cannot create opportunities for others to fill in the gaps about who you are. That means the responsibility to tell your story lies with you. That also means that you embrace and understand how your identity shows up in everything. Beginning with your identity is a good place to start.

Chapter 5

Find Transformative Allies

Allies

Allies are important for women of color at work. I have learned how allies play a role in the success of women of color. This statement has nothing to do with your ability to create your own destiny or your capacity or motivation to make things happen in life. To the contrary, your knowledge, competence, and resilience got you where you are today. Allyship is not about women of color, per se.

Allyship is an opportunity for your supporters to become a better version of themselves. In doing so, becoming an ally invites people who know you to stand with you. To pay attention to the experiences of women of color more closely. Allyship involves being honest about privilege; paying attention to what privilege looks like and how privilege is distributed.

Allyship with women of color happens when colleagues take action to support and advocate for women of color peers. There is an independent willingness to disrupt the status quo and a loyal effort to intervene when needed. There is a gesture to show solidarity. There is a commitment to be an advocate. There is an opportunity to use their privilege to benefit the whole. Allies are people in dominant positions who choose to disrupt their own comfort and security for the sake of equity and righteousness with the woman of color in their life. They work for anti-racism.

Allyship invites colleagues and friends to observe, judge, and then take action on how society has provided an uneven distribution of access, resources, and opportunities. This uneven distribution of resources benefits some and leaves others behind. Allyship requires willing colleagues and friends to unlearn behaviors that marginalize women of color and then act upon newfound knowledge and awareness to doing something about it.

Allies are people who are willing to use their social capital in service with others. Allies deploy their own resources in the service of, and in solidarity with, women of color. In this manner, they unite themselves with people of color, and more specifically, women of color. Relationships are central in allyship and should be mutually beneficial. However, it is not about what the woman of color can give to the ally for an equitable process to commence.

Allies become key partners in creating environments for women of color to be recognized.

An ally will instruct you on what you should be doing next to be successful in the organization and make you aware of threats to your success. All the while they run organizational interference on your behalf through exposing to others binary, racist, classist and sexist modus operandi that exist within the DNA of the culture, attempting to clear the pathway for your ascent.

Allies will stand with you during difficult times and engage in solidarity beyond their personal interest. An ally doesn't just get to say I'm an ally because it makes that individual feel good. A true ally has skin in the game. It costs something to be an ally.

It is critical to your success that you find the right people to be your allies. You have to find individuals who are interested in being an ally for the right reasons. That doesn't mean that it's always perfect; as people are imperfect. In knowing this, you will likely engage in what is known in critical race research as interest convergence.

In the context of allyship, interest convergence describes what happens when people with influence and power decide to support people different than themselves as an inherent benefit for them to do so. Interest convergence is a relational phenomenon. Not all allies operate under interest convergence. An ally operating within interest convergence thinking might subconsciously say, "I'm hoping that others see my commitment to helping a woman of color in my department."

You may be thinking that the concept of interest convergence is another unfair advantage for the privileged ally who benefits more from the relationship. There is a problematic notion in the concept of interest convergence that seems inauthentic. Being realistic in expectations of what an ally can do on your behalf is an important fact to anticipate.

Even the best-intentioned allies can find themselves seeking something in return whether they acknowledge this or not. Recognition for being a social justice advocate or feeling good for being a social justice warrior is a top reason why someone would want to become your ally. It can take years for an ally to unlearn and unpack what it means to be a true ally for you. You will need to decide how to intertwine your interest with theirs for a win-win situation.

Build Bridges

Women of color need other women of color to be their allies. One of the beautiful outcomes from building relationships with other women of color are the spaces created where you're not judged for everything you say or do. This creates trust and familial bonding that are important for women of color. Networking among women of color is empowering.

In May 2006, Catalyst released the report "Connections that Count: The Informal Networks of Women of Color in the United States" in order to examine barriers to the advancement of women in the workplace. Catalyst research revealed that a lack of access to networks of more influential colleagues was a major impediment for women in general but was more pronounced in the case of women of color because they face the racial barrier as well as a gender barrier.

This study brought to light two different strategies for networking that relate to allyship. It cites "blending in vs. sticking together" as strategies employed in the workplace. The first strategy looked at how a woman of color establishes relationships with those in power, primarily white and/or male, in a business or employment setting, with less interaction with other women of color. The second strategy suggested how women of color seek informal networks made up of colleagues racially or ethnically similar to themselves. In the study, Asian American women had a higher percentage of white males in their networks, opting for the "blending in" strategy. Latinas used a combination of the two with a large number of white males in their networks but with over 50 percent being women. African American women, in contrast, had the highest number of racially similar persons in their networks and the highest number of racially similar women pointing to "sticking together" as their preferred option.

The study went on to cite that when African American women are successful they don't appear to benefit from being viewed as insiders, and that networking with other African American women was connected to positive promotion rates. The study concludes that women of color should not be limited to networking with their own race nor feel obliged to network exclusively with colleagues who do not share their cultural heritage.

Women of color benefit from a combination of ally relationships: with white and/or male colleagues and with a community of women of color colleagues who share their gender and race experiences.

Not Every One Can Be Your Ally

Not everyone wants to be an ally to a woman of color. This includes people in positions of influence and authority who could be an ally yet are apathetic, disengaged, fearful, or not invested in your professional growth. My counsel to you is to not spend time on these individuals. Depending on your cultural background and upbringing, it can be hard to ask for help in the first place so reserve energy for the people who care. You have too many other important people and issues that require your attention. Plus, it takes time to develop and nurture relationships with your true allies. Do not waste precious energy on those who aren't equipped nor willing to support and love you.

The Harvard Business Review published an article by Maura Cheeks on March 26, 2018, titled "How Black Women Describe Navigating Race and Gender in the Workplace," where she explores the experiences of African American women before they reach the top leadership positions. Interestingly enough, she reports that all the women she interviewed spoke about the need to have someone in your corner, a sponsor, an ally. One woman interviewed went so far as to say, "If you have no one in your corner you get weeded out."

Transformative Allyship

I want to share with you an organizational diversity concept I developed and later expanded with my colleague, Ria DasGupta, in what we refer to as transformative allyship:

Transformative allyship is a highly committed form of allyship. Transformative allyship is when an individual leverages significant social, political, and economic capital to take action and risk loss of their own capital, if needed, to concentrate support for persons who are marginalized, underrepresented, and oppressed.

The relationship is affirmative and transformational. The ally observes injustice, makes a judgment about the injustice, and then takes action to correct the injustice.

The transformative ally spends their own capital in order to put that (marginalized, underrepresented) individuals' interest in the spotlight. The transformative ally makes sure their peers become aware of the reality and impact of them being marginalized. The transformative ally will use their social capital to create a more level and fair playing field through leveraging their influence and authority.

Transformative allies are committed to ensuring that you become visible to the right people. Transformative allyship goes further than the idea of sponsorship. Transformative allyship is a relationship that is mutually beneficial and disrupts gender inequity and racial inequality in whatever form it exists. Transformative Allies recognize the accompanying unequal outcomes women of color experience due to inequality and they leverage and expend their influence to disrupt and hold others accountable.

Transformative allies are the leaders in their industry or organization. They are founders and CEOs, mid-level persons to front line workers. The key here is the influence they wield and the authority and impact they have with others.

Transformative allies will make the invisible visible to people in their circles on behalf of women of color.

Coach an Ally

Allyship is social justice work in action. In my experience, it can take years of self-discovery for a white ally to transform themselves into warriors for social justice as they work against their privilege. Women of color are key actors in translating and making plain for allies what is gender and racial equity. There are displays of denial, fragility, self-preservation, and self-interest. There is anger, frustration, and tears. Disrupting privilege in organizations is difficult work.

Allyship is difficult work as the ally becomes aware of their own part to maintain gender and racial privilege. Allies need to develop their own support network with other allies. Women of color are uniquely positioned to give the feedback and support they need. Nurturing and supporting allies is an emotional labor that takes a tax and toll on women of color in organizations.

Transformative allies need women of color to be in their lives. This requires our love and perseverance if we choose to nurture and coach a friend or colleague. Here is why: Transformative allies are actively resisting conditioned messaging that says some people are worth more than others. They are resisting their own privilege. They are resisting institutional racism. They are resisting the opportunity they have to just sink into their own comfort and advantage. We know that allies make mistakes and at times disappoint. Transformative allies are part of a larger web of humanity and righteous solidarity in which the leadership and power of women of color emerges. Developing a supportive partnership with your transformative ally is important to fulfilling your purpose to become an agent of light and love in whatever you are being called to do.

Encourage Your Ally to Do Their Own Work

Part of supporting allies is to encourage them to do their own work of discovery and uncovering racism and sexism in their life. You should plan to communicate with them what you need and want and why it's important for them to care and act on your behalf. At times the relationship building process is tough as authenticity and telling the truth demands vulnerability on both sides.

It's harmful to your success if you never feel vulnerable and the same should go for your ally. Vulnerability is part of the process as the relationship needs to become transformational. One of the reasons we used the term transformational allies is because both you and your ally are becoming new people, together. You are in communion transforming through the lens and experiences of gender and race.

Conversely, allies become vulnerable with the women of color in their life as they step away from their privilege and expend amounts of personal capital that may feel uncomfortable for them. Your ally is working against unconscious messages about who she is in the world in relation to who you are in the world, messages that communicate your humanity is not equal to her humanity.

Both of you have put yourselves on the line. Both of you are working against hegemony and misogynistic forces. Both of you are confronting the status quo.

Love your friends and colleagues who are your transformative allies in whatever form and demonstration that seems best and encourage them often as they work for equity and inclusivity. Together, you're advancing the cause of social justice right where you are.

White Women and Women of Color

Although women of color and white women share gendered experiences, white women can't fully comprehend the racialized realities for women of color. White women do make strong allies for women of color. Yet, there are challenges that are best faced with openness and honesty in this relationship. It's one of the most powerful and most complex ally relationship at the same time. Allyship for white women and women of color is complicated, considering social and historical context. Here is why.

In society, white women's proximity and relationship to white males is close and strong. They, too, are deeply impacted by the misogyny of the dominant culture and its patriarchy. At the same time, their position in society and the privilege enjoyed in organizations and society exists due to how close their relationships are with white males. They enjoy the preferential option extended to them solely based on their race and relationship to white male influence and power. All forms and expressions of racism are seen (and felt) by women of color in their lives whether it comes from a man or woman. Women of color are adept in identifying and locating racism while it's occurring when white peers completely miss what happened.

In a way, even white female allyship can play out and reinvent legacies of patriarchy and whiteness. This is an unconscious blind spot that impacts how far they can go toward becoming transformative allies with women of color. White women are the most unlikely to act upon allyship in the most meaningful way for women of color as unconscious forms of racism plays out in subtle and implicit ways that are unknown to them. This is particularly the case for cisgender, middle to upper class, and liberal-minded white women.

From my years of inclusivity work and diversity research I wonder if there is an instinctive response that's happening with white peers to protect their privileged place and status in society and the workplace.

What I know for sure is that caring allies must continually commit to uncovering hidden assumptions and embedded biases that occur at the expense of any woman in the workplace and society, yet especially for women of color. All allies are called to become more aware and conscious of blind spots and commit to doing better.

For white colleagues reading this chapter, I challenge you to have a profound conversation with a woman of color in your life and whom you work with. Both of you can create a non-judgmental and sincere atmosphere that allows for the two of you to talk person to person. Ask the woman of color to honestly share her experiences with work place inequities including microaggressions from white peers who were completely unaware of their racialized transgressions. Find out her story. Make sure you are listening wholeheartedly.

Then, share with the woman of color your known privileges, shortcomings and invite her to give feedback. Your goal is to become conscious to the unknown behaviors you and other white females may be practicing unknowingly and unintentionally. Yet have the courage to accept that you more than likely made a hurtful impact and never knew it. This will be the beginning stages of forming an allyship with a woman of color.

For women of color, I challenge you to be open and believe in the power of transformative allyship and the possibility that any woman in your life who wants to change for the better, has the capacity to do so. Have a conversation with your potential transformative ally. Ask her to share what she is most afraid to tell you, especially race and inclusion, and learn more about what drives and feeds her fear of talking about or addressing issues of race.

Transformative allyship is delayed when vulnerability, honesty, and truth are absent. Resistance enters.

Resistance comes in many forms; through debate, through reasoning, through tears, through silence, through rejection, through blame. Professor Karen Dace edited an anthology documenting the narratives of women of color with their white female peers at work as they worked toward building authentic allyship and the difficult conversations had along the way. To overcome anything, you must be able to confront and acknowledge the possibility of your involvement or part in it.

Confronting racism with people we work with is difficult yet it's necessary. This makes transformative allyship a slow and worthwhile process as we do this together to mend and heal broken parts of our society, by forming one transformative relationship at a time.

The more intersectional experiences a white female has, affords her a better chance at transformative allyship with women of color. Queer and gender non-conforming people, women with disabilities, a parent of a Black or brown child, or women who have experienced the inequity of poverty, particularly as children themselves, can draw upon their intersecting marginalized identities to activate transformative allyship.

In the end, all individuals working toward fairness and justice bring baggage and need grace and support to make sense of it all, to unpack and lighten their load. White women and men who demonstrate a higher consciousness for social inequalities have the sensitivity necessary to care and do something about what's happening with women and persons of color at work and beyond. Reach out to them to invite dialogue and mutual understanding for taking action.

Allyship with Males

Males who commit to being open, having continuous learning experiences, and then acting on that knowledge, can stand with women of color as an ally. If he decides it matters to him, if he decides to unlearn untruths he was taught, and if he decides he has a responsibility and must do something with his privilege; allyship happens.

It's important to remember that influential white males were responsible for creating and sustaining the condition of racism and sexism in society as it exists. We thereby acknowledge the special duty and role white males have to actively end racism and gender inequality.

Conversely, for allyship with women of color to exist, influential white males and men of color must take responsibility to disrupt, dismantle, and reverse racism and gender inequity for all women and take firm and symbolic action when a situation involves a woman of color. Male allies do this publicly when needed to send a message to others that time is up for misogynistic and racialized behaviors which are unwelcome and wrong.

I believe taking on an active, symbolic leadership stance is the singular most important allyship role an influential and powerful male can make. White male allies are particularly well positioned, as they hold the highest percentage of corporate executive roles, to end toxic organizational and workplace culture and their accompanying behaviors where they are situated that have disproportionately impacted and hurt women of color.

By attending to the experiences and outcomes of women of color as an articulated focus, the experiences and outcomes of all persons and identities across the organization or corporate entity are improved.

Characteristics of Great Allies

When looking for allies, you want to look for individuals with both power and influence. These persons are natural choices to seek out as they already have positional authority within the organization. What that person says about you, whether informal or formal, will send a message to others.

Transformative allies will cause a shift in how others treat and regard your work within the industry.

In the same vein, identify and spend time with individuals who show a capacity and willingness to call out or address social justice issues and could become a transformative ally for you. Schedule time together to learn who they are and what they believe. Great allies are social justice minded and may not fit a label or description. You cannot judge a person until you get to know who they are. They may or may not be visibly engaged on issues that impact your success, per se, but they can become an agent of change on your behalf.

What does social justice minded mean or look like? It's a compassionate colleague who shares your values. People will always give us clues to who they are and what matters to them. These individuals are your natural allies whether or not you know it or they know it. These colleagues can be extremely effective at addressing issues of gender and racial inequity if they had more information and encounter experiences. Over time, conversations with that compassionate colleague can help to develop a powerful advocate for the issues that matter to you—and matter to the colleague.

The key is activating consciousness and awareness to the experiences of women of color in the organization. This occurs by telling your story and listening to theirs.

A Reflection on Transformative Allyship With a White Executive Woman

What steps have you taken to learn about Transformative Allyship?

The first step of transformational allyship for me is acknowledging that I have attained the position I have in part because of the way I look, the way I come across, the way I talk, where I'm from, and the college I attended. My race, class, educational background, my family structure—are all judged positively in my culture and in my workplace, in particular. I am a beneficiary of a system that privileges white, upper middle class, heterosexual, non-disabled women. The first step of being an effective ally for me has been to recognize and own that I have advantages and an entre in our society and in my workplace for things that have nothing to do with how hard I have worked or my particular gifts and talents.

What flows from that is a responsibility to name my privilege when I can. Likewise, I have a responsibility to point out when my colleagues are not taken seriously or when their words are misconstrued or misunderstood because they don't share those same advantages. I have had to learn (and am still learning) how to gently point out when a colleague's words are being misconstrued, misinterpreted, or simply ignored out of prejudice and unconscious bias. This is a challenge because we are not taught how to contradict our peers and superiors. One has to overcome the fear of embarrassment or retaliation to find the voice to speak up against bias in a new way.

Fundamental for me is remembering why I care. I don't want to live in a world when certain people are targeted by the police but not others, where Black children are many times more likely to be poor or go to jail. I have a personal stake in this fight because I don't like the way things are. This isn't about individuals getting bigger promotions or social accolades because of a commitment to diversity; it's about making a better world for myself and my children. Ultimately none of us is immune in a system that oppresses.

What has helped you to become a transformative ally?

I had the opportunity to participate in professional development offered through my employer—white women and women of color in conversation. I was shocked to hear about the experiences of my fellow staff women of color. Things I thought could never happen. That was a humbling experience for me. I was embarrassed to hear my colleagues had had terrible experiences of feeling excluded, ignored, de-legitimized, and that I had sometimes been a part of it.

The other experience was a professional development series offered through my employer on white identity development and white supremacy. It was eye-opening to learn that white supremacy and whiteness go hand in hand with racism. I never understood that before. I had thought of white supremacy as a small, fringe, violent group, associated with Nazis. I didn't understand that in the United States, white supremacy is a much more pervasive and mainstream ideology and that most of us white people are participating in its' perpetuation, consciously or not. The classes offered at work demystified white supremacy for me, allowed me to see my own internalized racism, and convinced me that I must call it out more plainly, particularly the ways in which it shows up as anti-Black bigotry. I became aware that it is my responsibility to call out white supremacy in a white culture.

Reflection:

Mobilize the Transformative Allies in Your Life

Women of color need transformative allies to support, nurture, and co-create new pathways for success. Allies sit at tables of influence, power, and privilege that not enough women of color have at the moment. In some instances, women of color are at the same table yet need a deeper commitment of solidarity from an ally peer. In your organization, search out those who have a sensitivity for issues on social justice: spend time with them, learn about them, engage in active dialogue with them. Your relationship with an ally is conscious as both of you become your higher selves in service to a greater calling of love, respect, and mutual reciprocity. This happens only through transformative allyship. When we transform our relationships at work and do a level of good for someone else that requires empathy, the outcome invites and enacts our highest humanity.

Chapter 6

The First Revolution Is Internal

Pain Behind the Triumph

Having earned a string of accomplishments gained over time that demonstrate I know how to be successful in my life and career is what others deem important. Perhaps those accolades show a commitment to setting goals and an ability to push beyond limitations. I would suppose all of these statements are true.

However, how do I calculate and account for the impact of internal work that led to healing processes in my mind, body, and heart which protected and saved me from the spirit-crushing realities of racism and sexism? Do external accolades, recognition, or achievement signal to others that you are whole in your life as a woman of color? How can you account for the effects of existing racialized or other identity related trauma reinforced on a daily basis in your environment? What do women of color leaders do with the steady and cumulative stream of microaggression experiences they've had and have held within their mind and body over years? Whose responsibility is it to make the work environment a whole place for women of color? Does anyone realize that women of color in organizations are suffering from racism and misogyny? What about people of color who live with and carry trauma from society—is it their job to keep it all stuffed to themselves when they are confronted with even more racialized and misogynic trauma at work? It's difficult to address or measure one's emotional and spiritual need using any form of a traditional organizational performance or assessment metric.

The accolades are wonderful as a visible manifestation and helpful reminder. I'm reminded that I am fierce and venerable as a Black woman and as a leader. Yet those accomplishments conceal the pain behind the triumph.

Self-Reflection Is Your Power Tool

This may be the most important chapter so I want you to read this carefully. Self-reflection and awareness are a power tool for you to become the leader you are meant to be. In context of leadership and power for women of color, self-reflection is a passageway to introspection and consciousness raising necessary to work through and against the impact of gender inequity. Self-awareness, in my view, is the key to being confident and powerful at work.

When we think of a tool we may think of a pair of scissors or perhaps a hammer as a common household tool. I want you to think of self-reflection as your power tool in the same way—you will go to and use this extraordinary practice everyday of your life.

Story: Yoga as Intervention

The moment of clarity happened in my doctor's office. I was there for a visit concerned about edema in my legs, and I just wanted it to go away. My weight was an indication that things were off. Walking up the hills and stairs of San Francisco, I would find myself out of breath and noticed I was not quite as physically limber.

Usually when my doctor walks into the room we'd greet one another with joy and admiration. He had been my physician since I first arrived to San Francisco. We had things in common. He was an alum of the university I work at and we always had great small talk getting him caught up on campus life. Our rapport was further strengthened by the communal aspect of being in the presence of another professional of color. My doctor is Filipino American and we both grew up in California and had similar childhood experiences.

The first words out of his mouth during this visit were that he wanted to know what was going on. Of course, he was referring to the presenting issue, the edema, that caused me to set up the appointment in the first place. Yet his communication was stern and caring at the same time. We both knew what he meant by the serious look he was giving me.

He declared that "my numbers" were the worst I'd ever had—that my weight was high for my height and frame, my blood pressure was particularly low. The edema itself concerned him, yet his integrated approach wanted more answers. We commenced into a detailed conversation about the stressors in my life. He delved into more of the specifics of my work. As a man of color who had successfully navigated his education and career, he understood why diversity work was important.

My doctor ordered a battery of tests that would assist him to assess and respond accordingly to the medical situation presented. Before I left his office with all my instructions and lab dates, I began to cry. I knew that my body literally had been holding onto stress and anxiety. My own, yet the anxiety and stress of others as well. People who freely shared their pain with me.

My physician and I talked about finding a meditative practice that could I easily incorporate in my life. We talked about walking and jogging. We talked about trying out a CrossFit or boxing gym. He said he's seen success among clients who took up yoga. That weekend I found a hot yoga studio. I checked it out and decided to join up on the spot. After suffering through my first class I thought I might have temporarily lost my mind. Yet I liked the interesting and diverse community of people who were members of the studio. And I loved how my body felt after the workout and sweat.

I lost thirty pounds in two years and the edema went away. I learned how to breathe deeply. Little did I know that yoga would help me to meditate and reflect on internal struggles. I continue to show up on my yoga mat three to four times a week if I can.

Us women of color should engage in quality introspective practices and processes. This may take the form of a mindfulness practice such as meditation, yoga, walking, prayer, or being in community with like-minded and like-hearted people. Reflective work is important as it leads to and creates wholeness in our lives. The byproduct is a sense of internal strength, vulnerability, and grace.

Reflection work matters as a counter to the visceral impact of institutional forms of racism and gender inequity. Without being fully aware, there is a toll women of color experience in pursuit of becoming successful in a traditional workplace environment. Reflection invites us to measure our success based upon what is good and valuable to us.

Women of color need to define and discover their own interior modes of engagement for awareness, fulfillment, and healing. This is what success looks like.

A reflective practice invites you into a space to be, to unfold, and unravel the layers of disappointment, hurt, and fear leading toward your own transformation. You will discover as I did that your personal interior work is the most revolutionary thing you can do to disrupt the status quo of our institutions and traditional work place environments.

Women of color who are self-aware, confident, and who know their worth are revolutionaries.

This process of deep discovery and awareness through reflection can only happen when you place yourself at the feet of vulnerability. By doing so, you get to release the things in your life that you have had little or no control over; and to submit to your shortcomings and all the times you messed up pretty badly as you can't go back to fix or change.

Lesson on Reflection from My Sunday School Teacher

One of things I learned early as a girl in my church environment was to be aware and attuned to the voice inside. When I think back, especially now that I'm a higher education leader and professor, I know exactly what my Sunday school teacher was doing in her lesson plans from a pedagogical perspective. My Sunday school teacher used the stories of the people in the Bible to teach the children in class about our own lives. She used the stories within the scriptures to make the people in the Bible come alive to the children by focusing on the character's human traits—their hopes, fears, and desires. Those characters seemed like people we might have known because our teacher made them seem real and relevant to us. They had a life, they had families, they had interests, they had jobs, and they always had a personal dilemma of some sort that involved other people in their lives.

I will venture to say her desired learning outcomes for her students in the Sunday School class were three-fold: 1) to teach her students key life principles through biblical characters in a way that was accessible and relevant to her students' lives; 2) to make meaning connections through the lives and choices made by the actors in the scriptures to inform her students' character development; and 3) to teach us about human nature and to be conscious of our thoughts and actions.

This early exposure gave me a foundation to begin a life-long journey to want to know about my interior and spiritual self. I am grateful to my Sunday School teacher who served as an early instructional guide in teaching me about self-reflection as a teaching tool.

Reflection as a Balm for Unconscious Bias

As an executive woman of color, engaging my interior life has proved invaluable as I navigate the troubled waters of our workplaces and guide others in their navigation as well. I think of reflection as a balm that can soothe the emotional effects of daily slights associated with gender and race together; as a salve to calm anxiety and pressure. The reality of our workplaces demands for us to be adept at code switching, to move with fluidity through diverse and challenging scenarios, and be politically aware in our engagements with peers.

I believe all professional women of color need a reflective and meditative practice to counter the impacts and heal the effects of unconscious biases, microaggressions, and cultural appropriation that we encounter regularly in our lives.

This past summer marks three years since I walked into that hot yoga studio having never done anything like that before. I did my research and had heard from others about the detoxifying aspects of the practice. To this day, I continue the practice of yoga. As a matter of fact, when I need to release mounting emotions that tiny piece of health and wellness real estate called my yoga mat is the only place where I can release anxiety, worry, and fear.

Needless to say, yoga is now part of the meditative practice that has changed my outlook and impacts every aspect of my life for the better.

To be your highest self at work requires that you are fully present and with others and mentally strong. A transformative and catalytic mindfulness practice is in order for the lives of busy and high-performing women of color.

For you, a daily meditation practice may be a walk through your favorite park or a hike nearby where you live. Your meditation engagement and joy may be from a beloved dog or cat whose presence calms your spirit, captures your heart, and makes you smile. Each person is different and the meditative style unfolds and takes shape with the individual.

Having an awareness and interior practice proves necessary when you encounter daily instances of unconscious and implicit bias among the people you work. Having an interior practice supports you as you work through instances of being overlooked at work and not given the opportunity to grow in the organization. Having an interior practice is a salve for your heart and soul as you work through frustration and feelings when your allies that you depend upon let you down. You will need a practice that is accessible and makes sense in your life.

Stillness, Breath, and Solitude

Each one of us needs to find a way to counteract all of the noise and movement that goes on around us. Where do you go to find stillness? How do you cancel out the noise and sensory overload each of us are bombarded with on a daily basis?

Living in San Francisco there are public spaces for reflection everywhere. There are many opportunities in the Bay Area and Northern California as well that I take advantage of as much as possible. When friends and family visit, we take them to the ancient Redwood Tree Forest in Muir Woods or walk with them through the beautiful grounds of the Presidio, both of which are part of the U.S. National Parks. I treasure National Parks and Yosemite is my destination of choice for its majesty and proximity within a day-trip excursion when needed.

I also began to look for ways to reconnect with my interior self. I needed to find community and to build community with women. I began my search and started attending Women's Retreats with a focus on women's career and spiritual development.

In more recent years, I discovered and found silent retreats as a powerful catalyst for quieting the noise that gets in the way of listening to the voice that's telling me what to do. Silent retreats were a bit of a luxury at first as you must plan the time to get away, yet as my daughters were older and had their own interests and commitments, I took advantage of the opportunity. For a 24-hour period or longer, I was invited into a meditative state of quiet. It seemed difficult at first but once I got past the first morning and then the afternoon, I knew I could do the quiet thing just fine. Personally, I enjoy a beautiful garden at any time of the year and the grounds of retreat centers are often lovingly stewarded with flowers, fountains, potted plants, trees, and nooks and corners for reading, thinking, walking, and praying in silence. Some retreat centers are near a body of water that adds an element of wonder and there are pathways for hiking.

Through retreat experiences I became surprised to learn what keeps my attention. And conversely, what distracts my attention. I had to face what I think about persistently throughout the day.

I think about the future a lot and things I have absolutely no control over. That means I wasn't spending time in the present. I think about interactions I had with others and what I would have said or done different if I had the opportunity to repeat. That means I waste my time on things I have no control over anymore. I think and role play in my head. I think about how things are unfair for certain groups and what I want to do about it. I think about racism in America. I think about people who get on my nerves. I think about the people I need to reach out to who give me energy, yet I haven't done so. I think about the health and welfare of my husband and daughters.

At the time, most of thoughts throughout the day are not useful or do not matter in the larger scheme of life.

The meditative practice and mindful framework of retreats is a revelatory process to becoming aware of your mental thoughts. Your mind is occupied by forces that prohibit your ability to access new ways of thinking and news ways of being. Your mind can be a battleground, especially for women of color dealing with experiences that have legacies of racial, gender, and social exclusion.

I have come to believe that there is this internal trickster who seeks to take up residence in my mind whose total purpose is to distract through confusion, worry, anxiety, and lies.

Who do you think you are? That's a thought thrown from the trickster. Can anyone truly love me? Again, the trickster. Am I good enough? Definitely, classic trickster in full effect. We carry trauma in our bodies and within our cells. Trauma among marginalized communities of color has a generational element that is passed down. The effects of traumatic experiences of women of color and the narratives of trauma that accompany them stay with us and follow us into the workforce as we take on leadership roles. The trickster knows all too well about our trauma—past and present.

———

An interview with a millennial woman of color on race and the power of breath

Noelle, Interior Designer
Noelle:

When I feel anxious at work, I focus on every single breath in that moment. That helps to break up the moments. If young women of color like me can really harness our breathing, we can get through anything. There are periods of time in which I find that I can't even breathe. Yet if I can just slow down and focus on being still and on my breath, I find that I am able to push through the moment.

For women of color like me, breathing and trying to be present in different moments can help out in a lot of things we experience, especially when things are going wrong. When you feel like nothing positive is coming out of your relationships or your work and things are not quite right in general.

There are too many Black women who think no one will want them as they are and that creates a level of anxiety and can feel like failure. I think that's crazy. If we as women of color take a step back and breathe, focus on the moment. Realizing that every stage of our life is for a reason and just to live in that moment and not worry too much about things we have no control over. We can learn to be and to enjoy and just move into the next phase of our life.

Breathing and being present alleviates all those issues, yet I think it comes from a greater pressure that society puts upon women, and women of color are impacted at a higher level.

Mary:

What would need to happen for you to increase your commitment to your interior meditative life and invest in your mindfulness?

Noelle:

Routines are really important. Something that is stable and regular is necessary.

For you it's yoga. If something happens [to you] there is always a place you have that you can go to for a release. That's important for all women of color professionals to have. It doesn't need to be everything but having a moment of time that you can block out in your schedule that eliminates all the noise in your life is really beneficial instead of creating a plan that's not very doable. There is a ton of things in life that will bring you stress.

If you can just take a designated period of time for yourself it's better in the long run.

Mary:

How do you manifest reflection practically so you can show up fully present at school or work?

Noelle:

Having those still times on your own. And once you can isolate yourself, you may realize that you like being with others or vice versa. Then when you are at work, focus on those same things you enjoy. If you like people, then try to spend as much of your job engaging with others. Create a workspace that supports your spirit and who you are and how you operate.

For me, I do design consulting and there's an aspect of my job I don't like. Yet there is an aspect of my work I absolutely adore where I get to create things. As long as you spend the time to find out what you like, even at work, and apply those principles it will make your experience richer at work; you will reach your goals and manifest things that are good such as success.

Reflection:

Self-Reflection in Community

As I travel regularly to other parts of the country, there are many opportunities to find community and be with others. There is personal and emotional healing among people who see you and who can feel you. Social media platforms are brilliant in capturing and collecting information for people who want reflective experiences in community and helps them find one another. Try to connect to life-giving opportunities that go beyond everyday consumption and consumerism of goods and services. Find other women of color of like mind and like interest for a collective healing experience.

In the months ahead, I plan to attend my first yoga retreat and am excited about what that new experience will bring to my interior life engagement and overall health and well-being.

I urge you to find and attend an experience that interests you and connects you in a meaningful way to your interior life.

Chapter 7

Speak Truth to Power: Use Your Voice and Tell the Truth

"If they don't give you a seat at the table, bring a folding chair."
– Shirley Chisholm

Silence Is Negligence

Being courageous at work and using your voice in service for others is a calling. Speaking up to address inequality in the workplace and society both for themselves and others is a calling that women of color have consistently answered for as long as the American workforce has existed.

The leadership of women of color is intertwined with truth telling, and doing so with conviction. Telling the truth is a key trait and the ultimate responsibility of leadership. By truth telling, women of color use their voices to help others see the invisible, those parts of our existence that are often overlooked.

Building your organizations' capacity for engaging the truth and doing it in a manner that keeps people engaged is an integral part of your calling. Every time you speak up on the side of what's right and good you teach others through example. Modeling for others is the ultimate form of demonstrative leadership on issues that matter: empowering others to learn about your vision and what you know to be true.

Telling the truth for women of color is confronting harmful narratives and stories that are repeatedly told and acted upon over and over again.

Truth and Reconciliation

Truth is a basic requirement for reconciliation to fully emerge. The two principles, truth and reconciliation, go hand-in-hand and are mutually dependent upon one another. To reconcile, there is a change in the relationship that brings two groups of people together after a period of discord. Reconciliation brings together what had been apart from one another.

There is an on-going need for truth and reconciliation processes in all American organizations.

For evidence, look no further than the compensation gap for women versus men in the workforce; look at the persistent dominance of white males across every major leadership role in nearly all fields and industries; and then look at the dearth of women who have senior leadership roles in companies or who have become directors on corporate boards. If you intersect the data on gender and add the data on race to the equation, the facts speak for themselves: it is clear that women of color are at the bottom quartile of every economic metric based on prosperity and career advancement in the United States.

In February 2018, Catalyst released a new report entitled "Day-to-Day Experiences of Emotional Tax Among Women and Men of Color in the Workplace." Catalyst Vice President of Research Dr. Dnika J. Travis, Ph.D. said, "Women of color continue to deal with some of the workplace's most entrenched hurdles such as pay inequities and near invisibility in top leadership roles, as well as daunting roadblocks that stifle the meaningful dialogue that would help make real progress. Over time, these daily battles take a heavy toll on women of color, creating a damaging link between their health and the workplace."

Disparities anywhere create an unequal and uneven circumstance for communities everywhere.

And so, the organizations we work for have unequal and uneven realities embedded within their structure and therefore within their DNA. The realities of uneven outcomes create differing experiences for women and people of color in general. At the nexus of these two, gender and race, the research proves how women of color are the ones who are impacted the most. For more than thirty years since the first McKinsey study, corporate America has made little progress in improving women's representation at every level and women of color are the most underrepresented of all categories.

Women of color have always had to use their voice and tell the truth whether or not it was allowed. This truth telling role continues within our workplaces and dates back over centuries. Historically, when the opportunity for us to speak was not afforded, we mustered our strength and courage to push forward ideas of fairness and justice often at the risk of personal harm.

We told the truth in spite of the risk. We told the truth for ourselves. We told the truth for our children and families. We told the truth for the children and families of others. We did this with the purpose and intent to make things better and right. You have a legacy of courage within you to bring forward concerns of injustices that impact everyone around you—which in turn improves the leadership and integrity of your organization.

A Conversation on Using Your Voice for Change

I had a coaching session with a retired executive woman of color and discussed the experiences of the incoming generation of women of color leaders in the workplace. "There are two cultures that are coming up against each other at work and they've never interacted before." She was talking about the cultural experience of women of color and the patriarchal culture we see at traditional places of employment.

We had an informative and insightful discussion on how women leaders who bring culturally-informed identities into their leadership practice are challenging the homogenous nature of work environments in meaningful and exciting ways. Reflecting on her experiences, she noted that there has to be some conceding on the part of the dominant culture to create space for new ways of leading and knowing that women of color in leadership are offering; and that a culture shift is required.

This made me think about the role women of color play in shaping and molding corporate culture through the process of truth telling.

What if truth telling became a valuable part of a company's identity in how they do business? How can we create inclusive and empowering organizations without wanting to know the truth? How can we solve the intractable and difficult problems in the absence of speaking the truth? How can an organization be truthful in the absence of having women of color at each level of leadership?

We discussed how the veteran executive found herself at times taking on a different voice (other than her own distinct voice) to be heard—maybe trying to be like the men around her. She wanted to be taken seriously. We talked about what happens to the heart and soul of women of color when they take on personal characteristics that are not their own.

"You feel like a part of you is lost: creating a sense of anxiety about being in your own skin in the workplace," she shared.

Insight emerged as we discussed the need for leaders to understand and create space for women of color by acknowledging their value and contribution. "Someone has to give up something for the other side to emerge," she stated. "And from what I see, the dominant work culture wants the culturally-informed ways of being in the workplace to go away all together. It's like assimilating into a patriarchal work environment is the unstated goal here."

Hearing her statement made me think about how much we need to reimagine and rethink how we approach our decision-making teams and what we currently have in place. We have constructed a limited and finite number of seats available at the table of leadership. We've created a zero-sum understanding and response to deciding who sits at the table. With such a limited number of seats available, the voices of women of color are being locked out by design.

We have thousands of important tables that are absent the voice of a woman of color. Our communities and our world are suffering as a result to their missed leadership.

A commitment to truth telling would require a company to use a new math—the whole is greater than the sum of its parts. Inclusivity does not mean that one individual or group must lose for another to gain. This is a reductionist approach to inclusivity.

Emergent thinking would call for us to build organizational capacity for truth telling and inclusivity that creates a larger table. Companies and organizations that value truth telling simply must make the room for it. They add women of color to every single important decision-making table that exists by deciding to change their limited thinking and construct a new table that is inclusive.

————————

That's the primary reason why women of color must continue to be the leaders who speak up wherever they are located to ignite the right issues until smart companies start seating them in their rightful place. Some companies will be leaders and set the tone for others. They understand women of color speak directly to issues that impact the nature of what is prioritized and responded to.

We can't assimilate into the background and pretend we are not aware of issues. There are other leaders who do that. Women of color do not assimilate in organizations. Women of color do not shrink back when issues are difficult.

Women of color lead the way for others by clarifying what is important and what deserves our attention.

I encourage you to work against the patriarchy wherever you are by telling the truth as an act of love and courage for the people you care for. The history of people of color in America is to make the invisible visible for others to see. We must push the conversation or the truth will never emerge.

————————

Speak Truth to Power

An organization's culture is a mutually re-enforcing element to the quality or detriment of any person's workplace experience. A misaligned organizational culture becomes even more exasperating for women of color at work due to the intersection of gender and race. Women of color will either thrive or struggle within an organization dependent upon and related to how well the mission and values of the organization align with her lived experience at work. This means, how is inclusivity practiced as a realized element of organizational life?

There has to be enough congruence in what the workplace says is important to what actually happens with the people who work there. The environment cannot be inclusionary for some or exclusionary for others. It's essential that mission and organizational climate come into alignment for mission-centered organizations to fulfill their purpose and to thrive.

Women of color are equipped to bring the organization into better alignment through a focus on truth telling with intention. This process of supporting mission alignment is a form of organizational truth telling. Women of color course correct and help organizations fulfill their mission and purpose. They do this when they urge companies to pay attention to who is disproportionately impacted by policies and how they are implemented. They do this by bringing forward ideas and information on how everyday practices impact people differently. Women of color bring an acute understanding of what structural oppression is and how power and privilege manifests in the everyday aspects of business operations.

The organizational culture also determines the degree to which unconscious and implicit bias is tolerated or mitigated. Or conversely, the way unconscious and implicit bias is actually acknowledged and then dealt with and handled. The more you know about the culture of an organization, the more you understand how much truth telling is required to bring the company into alignment with its cultural values ensuring that all may thrive. It's important to understand the character of the organization where you are employed and what kind of organization you want it to be. This understanding will guide you to know how best to contribute and how to use your voice. Your organization is better due to your presence and leadership.

Advocate for Yourself

There are always windows of opportunities to tell the truth. Knowing when and how to seize those moments is important. The number of women of color in leadership roles is low and there are few allies who will take the risk to speak up on your behalf. There are times you tell the truth when you shouldn't have to.

Be mindful that others are taking note of how and when you use your voice. You will have to advocate and speak up for yourself when it's too important not to and when no one else does. Make sure you have your facts right. And when it's time for you to use your voice, communicate with confidence knowing that you bring with you a legacy of righteousness. Speak from that special place that only a woman of color can.

Interview: On Truth Telling
Alice, Gender Studies Major, UCLA
Mary:

You are a university student at one of the finest public universities in the world and you are speaking truth about the experiences of women of color on your campus. How are you learning to tell the truth?

Alice:

I'm just noticing here that girls speak about adversity and yet do not know what adversity means. My friend and I attended a conference here at UCLA about homelessness and she is Latina. During the conference another student said that, "Nobody is born homeless." My Latina friend turned to that person and responded, "Well, that's not true, because I was." She is also a student at UCLA. That's what it's like to tell the truth here as young women of color. We find ourselves constantly educating others about what it means to be Black or Latina or whatever.

Because the main idea is that people have different ideas on adversity. Some think adversity is not being able to run track for an event or they didn't get into UCLA the first time they tried. Things they can join at a later time or try again. People like me, and others like me feel that they have had a lifetime of adversity to even get into UCLA. It's like our very presence here is a testament that we know what adversity means. On a day-to-day basis, we are describing this or dealing with this issue of what adversity means, every day, and what our experience is and what the experience of others like us is.

I have used my voice here and spoken up about adversity in spaces when it's clear others don't know. In my women's study class, I speak up on things that I agree with from our readings and give my perspective and listen to others about the articles. I have been privileged coming from the home I have with my parents yet I have seen things as a child growing up (in Oakland) and have been exposed to difficult issues. And that makes me really grateful to be here because I didn't think that I ever would be here.

The same for the friends that I choose as they ascribe to the same sentiment of gratitude as I do. That sense of knowing where I came from and how fortunate I am to be here stays with me all the time in everything that I do. Even in my friends, I'm looking for people who care about the world and care about people who have not had the chances that we have—we all are women of color coming from our own challenges and backgrounds even when we were children. I know that I have a strong sense of other people's adversity that has been passed on to me.

Speaking quite honestly here, our truth is the only thing getting us by here. Because we don't know anyone else who has done this here, and the truth of our own existence by being here is what's getting us by.

Mary:

Just to hear you say that your truth is the only thing that is grounding you (at UCLA) it's the exact same thing Soujourner Truth said some 200 years ago.

Alice:

In my gender studies major I am learning that everything in feminism that matters really comes to this: The experiences of Black women, Latinas, Native American and other women of color, their adversity, and their will to change things. It's this combination of consciousness and advocacy that changes everything for all women, across all ethnicities/ race, class, and situation.

My question is why did it take so long for me to get here? We have to urge white women to use their privilege in a better manner so women of color can also get to the heights of achievement and inclusion.

I'm finding out now that being in college with a lot of white students and learning that they are clueless to how other people outside of their small experiences live. I've been surprised to learn just how much they do not know about people of color besides what they learn through the media and that they have no idea that they don't—and still they can be flippant and so self-assured about themselves and that they are so right about things.

It's been frustrating for me here. I feel as a young bi-racial woman that I'm going to be dealing with this stuff for a very, very long time, as we all will eventually become professionals in the workplace. That's unfortunate. These classmates are the professionals who will be running things someday. It makes me sad to see that progress takes so long.

I mean, when pretty smart and privileged white students my age still don't understand what racism is or they have little knowledge about poverty and other social issues that impact people different than them, and they are kind of cocky about it all and blind to their ignorance, it feels disheartening.

The main issue I have when we tell the truth is that you are either heard or you are not heard when we speak the truth. Because the issue is really what does your audience think they already know; whether we are talking about what adversity means and anything else. Their focus is on the thing they think they know and not hearing women of color who are telling them something different than their current knowledge base. And they don't want to hear it nor accept what you have to say—even though we are supposedly peers here at UCLA.

Mary:

What advice do you have for young women of color on speaking their truth?

Alice:

If you don't tell people what you want, you won't be able to further yourself. Read everything. And write.

Be passionate about what you care about. I was so embarrassed to say out loud that I was interested in Gender Studies. Everyone's view it seemed was that it wasn't a great idea. I finally talked with my academic advisor at my community college about it. I was holding tears back because I was so embarrassed to admit what I really wanted to major in. Once I told her she encouraged me to go for it and told me that there are communities of students studying social justice at UCLA and that was a good thing. I had been reading feminist novels and feminist things all along. My advisor found out and said it was OK and to be true to myself. I decided to apply to UCLA and just owned that this [being a gender studies major] is who I am and what I enjoy.

This is what I'm learning here for sure. Studying gender and race is like telling a fish about water. It's like everything that we think we know because it's all around us, yet it's clear that we don't see or know it at all.

Chapter 8

Enact Your Leadership

W hat are the everyday issues you will face as a woman of color who leads? How do you show up to lead? What is leadership?

Leadership is a nebulous notion and can be contradictory depending upon who's leading, who's following, and the overall situation. Exactly what does being a leader mean? As it stands today, our idea of leadership is informed by the media and what we see in front of us. Most of our images and ideas around leadership have been created by a homogenous and single narrative which is a danger. Who a leader is and what that person looks like, what language does that person speak, where they come from, and their approach is contextual, relational, and relative.

How do you know that you are a leader? The fact is that our view of leadership and power is remarkably narrow, contritely prescribed, and often misunderstood. All of my work on understanding leadership began during my childhood.

For me, leadership looks like my mother raising her children after unexpectedly losing her husband.

The Chevy

I was nine years old when my dad died. My mom had been traditional in that she worked in the home as a mother and a homemaker. She had five daughters, of which I was number four. My younger sister who was the baby was literally that when my dad passed away—she was only three years old at the time. There really is not much you can do when you are just old enough to know a tectonic shift has occurred in your life and there is nothing you can do about. I was still just a kid. You just have to go on with it. Which is what I've done in the reality of losing my father as a child.

We kept Dad's 1975 or '76 Chevy Impala that was parked most of the time and sat in the driveway under an awning. Although I wasn't allowed to drive until I turned eighteen, one of the fun jobs I got to do as a kid was to go outside and start up the car. I would just let it sit and run and press the gas a bit to keep the engine working. About a year or so had passed when I noticed that mom had made a decision.

I would accompany her to the classroom at the nearby high school. It turned out to be an adult driving education course. My mom had become a young widow at home with one school age daughter and another one getting ready for kindergarten. And a good car was sitting idle in her driveway. She needed to get her driver's license although she hadn't driven before. I recall the first time we walked to the high school together. It was a hot summer day and I remember sweating. The teacher took attendance. She instructed me to sit down at the desk behind her.

In what seemed like a basic driver's education course, of which it was, I saw her courage in that classroom. I brought an activity or coloring book with pencils each class period to occupy myself. I do not remember much else except a man speaking at the front of the class showing the occasional movie clip, using an overhead projector. I watched from behind my mom. She had a fill-in workbook as supplemental instructional material along with a book for the purposes of getting a California driver's license. The classroom itself was pretty unmemorable, unremarkable. A basic public high school environment.

I am pretty sure I witnessed the embodiment of being courageous when life is uncertain and unstable and what it looks like to take action by starting with oneself. There was a clear necessity that serves as a catalyst. Perhaps this is what we should call leadership.

Envelopes and Stamps

There was a day of the month when my mother would pull out her checkbook to pay the bills and gather envelopes and stamps. She would write out the checks, write the address in the upper left-hand corner, and ask me to lick and add the stamps to each envelope. I observed how Mom kept a ledger of the balance in her account by subtracting each check that had been written. Over time, when I was about twelve, she allowed me to take over some of the bill paying responsibility and I would write out the payments on the checks and write our information on the envelopes. She would sign each check and I would place the completed ones on the mailbox held by a clothes pen.

By the time I was thirteen, I knew how to collect all the bills and how to write out checks. In the late 1970s and early 80s the household payments went something like this: checks to the gas, telephone, and electric companies, check to the family doctor's offices (we had no medical insurance), sometimes a check to the family dentist (again, no dental insurance), check for the water bill to pay the city municipality, and a tithing check to support God's work at the church. There were more payments we prepared that were quarterly—like the property tax bill which was the largest one that I can remember and automobile insurance. Vehicle registration was only once a year and we always drove to the DMV office and paid the car registration in person at the DMV window. The lines then were not as long as they are now.

My mom did not use a calculator. Obviously personal digital assistants (PDAs), the precursor to the modern smart phone, had not yet been invented and she didn't have a handy aid to keep track or help her. Her financial world was cash money and personal checks with a simple hand-written ledger. She would inspect the checks I wrote and then sign them. I wrote our address on each envelope when we were done and licked the appropriate cost of delivery in stamps and clipped the freshly sealed payments to our home mailbox for the delivery man to pick up. For years, I witnessed her do this month after month.

Does my mom's financial mastery and keen ability to manage her household resources and pay all her bills on time, for years, and the capacity to stay within the black and not the red count as leadership? Does leading your family and finances after unexpected tragedy strikes, like losing your husband, and raising up two young girls alone count as leadership? Can her ability to set aside money each month on a limited pension and social security benefit from her deceased husband and then set aside resources each month for a savings account in the event of another emergency and still plan for the future, be an act of leadership?

This seems to me like behaviors often described in business school curriculum with terms like management, strategy, planning, forecasting, oversight, real world application, and vision. Is that what a leader does?

One more story to drive my point home.

Classrooms and More Classrooms

That girl who sat in the classroom at the local high school watching and waiting with her mother as she went back to school during a hot summer to learn how to drive and get her driver's license also went to many more classrooms over the course of her life. She would go to classrooms to earn a bachelor's degree. Then she would return again to attend more classrooms to earn a master's degree. Eventually she decided to return to school, like her mom, out of necessity and went back to the classroom once more to get her terminal doctoral degree.

The girl that sat under her mother's supervision to write out checks did not become an accountant or take up work in the field of finance. Instead she became a university executive, a leader in diversity, and a college professor teaching graduate business and doctoral level education students how to be leaders, and how to show up with courage and compassion in the workplace, among a few other things. Her awards include recognition for human rights advocacy for women and she grew up to oversee a $160M budget for one of the largest and most venerable public libraries in North America.

That girl, as you know, became me.

Does my mom's raising a future educator and executive who challenges presidents and CEOs of companies and teaches students that a commitment to diversity, equity, and inclusion count as an expression of leadership and love in the highest form? Does her contribution in raising me count as a contribution to the thousands of students her daughter has led and prepared as the next generation of leaders? Would my mother be profiled as a leader by any business journal or leadership magazine? Is her action what leaders are supposed to do?

Enact Leadership as Redefined by Women of Color

What is sorely lacking in the leadership narrative is the nuance, the sophistication, and the beauty that women of color encapsulate, embody, and bring each day to traditional and nontraditional workplaces. Their very being and essence are missed in our picture and vision of leadership as people look right past them. Their heart and the way they show compassion, empathy, and love to the people who need it the most go unacknowledged. Their courage and the brave manner in which they stand up to their own fears as well as responding to difficult and challenging situations in their environment in spite of adversity is not recognized.

How does a woman of color bring her phenomenal presence into the traditional status quo spaces in our society as powerful leaders? The fact is, you bring it with you by just showing up. You enact your leadership each day you walk into the office, the studio, the laboratory, and onto the field by embracing yourself fully.

My mother demonstrated competence, skill, and grace in the management of her household as a widowed woman with two young daughters at home and three older daughters transitioning to young adulthood. She found herself thrust into complete independence after her husband's sudden death. She found the courage to continue moving forward by taking on new challenges and engaging new opportunities.

She led herself, first, then she led her children. She enacted leadership through her own lived experiences of dealing with finances through crisis and managing a household of five daughters when a spouse was taken. She taught through behavior which was passed down and emulated by me. That was leadership and management in full effect.

Mom taught me 3 principles of enacting leadership:

- Leadership is an act of courage and faith
- Leadership is an act of unexpected preparation
- Leadership is an act of showing up and modeling for others even when you are not ready for prime time

Leadership is an act of courage and faith and a demonstration of what it means to be brave enough to confront the challenges of life. I learned what bravery was from my mother's example of leadership. She embodied what it takes to muster up all your strength in the face of fear, and possibly doubt, and still showed up with the presence and the vulnerability that's required to learn something completely new.

Leadership is an act of unexpected preparation. My mother was not expecting to become a leader. She didn't ask for it and from what I knew, did not seek it out. Yet leadership came to her and found her. Leadership identified her and appointed her. You master anything by spending the requisite time learning the task. It takes hours of doing the same thing over and over, then doing it again and again. This steady stream of repetition grounded in discipline builds up one's competence and skill that leads to mastery. Leadership is an act of modeling for others the attitudes, behaviors, and prerequisite skills necessary to be successful in any endeavor.

Leadership is an act of showing up and modeling for others even when you are not ready for prime time. My mother's instruction was about modeling behavior rather than talking and giving instruction. She showed me what leadership looked like demonstrated through her behavior when in a crisis situation and what she did to get through the crisis. So much was passed on through her modeling behaviors without ever saying a word.

Other Lessons on Leadership

Leadership is expertly balancing your check book and paying your bills on time each month with no fanfare and only consistency.

Leadership is being vulnerable by going back to school with a daughter in tow and showing up, again and again, all the while teaching valuable lessons of persistence and resilience to your child along the way. You lead and you teach by example.

Leadership is learning to drive for the first time in your forties.

I hope you sense that enacting your leadership is really about how you show up each day. Your actions have implications for those in your environment and have impact long after what's happening in the present is over. My mom was thoughtful to include me in her development and leadership processes; and in doing so, instructed me on how to continue my own learning and development.

Those early lessons could not be communicated or taught through an MBA program or business school curriculum. Primarily because those programs would not see my beautiful Black mother as the leader she was. There are real consequences to not seeing certain people as leaders. As children's rights activist Marion Wright Edelman said, "You can't be what you can't see." And Marion Wright Edelman was the first African American woman to pass the bar exam in Mississippi.

Enacting your leadership is a display of your resilience and grace when going through difficult periods and situations. Enacting your leadership will require that you go through the fire. This may take the form of missed opportunities and promotions that should have been yours. Or may entail unfair treatment that can impact your prosperity and sense of happiness. Yet enacting your leadership is worth you becoming who you are meant to be.

Whatever role or work you decide to pursue, remember you have a legacy of dignity, grace, and resilience as a woman of color. Hold on to your identity as your foundation and as an affirmation of who you are, where you come from, and what you are made of.

Chapter 9

Step into Your Power

Vulnerability is the first place you must go before you can truly step into your power. Author Brené Brown has helped us understand through her research that it's through the vulnerability where we find our confidence. Our power lies deep within waiting for us. Yet we must attend to the hurt, disappointment, fear, and anger so we may become the courageously powerful woman we've been longing for. The interior work must first be completed, allowing you to step into your power and become the powerful woman that lies within your core.

In my experience, stepping into your power required that I deal with my own trauma. I know this to be true, as I will explain in this chapter. And I know this is true from my work with other high-capacity talented women of color—whether they were students I advised or taught, or professional and executive women; all of whom had to walk the same path you are walking on.

My experience with trauma is knowing and dealing with my own. You will need to identify where you can get the support you will need to deal with trauma in your life. For me, trauma is where I found my truth. I found my truth through a meditative and healing practice, which for me was yoga. Trauma work can propel you into your power yet requires you spend the requisite time with healers and certified professionals.

I can recall the exact moment I stepped into my power. My power had been there all along and patiently waiting on my internal revolution to commence so that my personal power might emerge.

Yet what I know now that I did not know then is that I had too much trauma that needed to be acknowledged and attended to. There was real loss in my life. I had carried with me a beating, yet hurt, heart. I was conditioned to continue plugging right along in my fabulous, yet concealed, broken heartedness.

I carried it forth and brought broken heartedness with me.

First Trauma

We walked to church most Sunday mornings and back home the same way. It was common for me to skip ahead of my mother and sister, especially on the return home. I actually skipped or ran home and kept a steady one to two blocks lead ahead of my mother and sister because I was fast and because I could. It was after church anyways and I didn't have to worry so much about making sure my dress didn't get messed up from playing hard. I just had to be careful to not scratch up my patent leather church shoes.

I got home first, which was usual, and ran into the house looking to see where my dad was. He was there, sitting in his chair, sleeping. When I touched him to wake him up, he did not move. I shook just a bit and his body slumped downward. I am not sure all that I knew for sure, yet something was not right about this situation.

I was still a child yet somewhat old enough to grasp that he was gone. My hand was on his shoulder, still gently trying to see if he would wake up. I'm not quite sure how but I knew my father had gone from me. I stood there with him.

I heard the sound of the front gate open signaling that my mother and younger sister had arrived. I ran out of the house and reported to her before she could walk in to what I just saw. I remember the look on my mother's face.

It was a sunny and beautiful morning in Stockton, California. We had come from a great day of Sunday services: Sunday school classes for the children and then we came together in big church in the sanctuary with everyone. I sang with the children's choir that morning. We hung out just a bit after church, which was the best part because it was sort of a social time as people chatted and I talked. I played with my friends before we all departed.

Mom sent me across the street to our neighbor Mr. Phil to help out. He called the authorities. The fire department came first and then the paramedics. We had never had the big red fire truck come to our home before, yet I'd seen it before in the neighborhood.

A small group of parishioners had pulled their cars over, as we happen to live near the church, and they were headed home from service when they saw the medical vehicles at our home. A group of neighbors had also gathered. I held open the front screen door as the fire personnel and paramedics poured inside. I watched them attend to my father. At some point, I remember a fire fighter stood up and I can remember feeling a hand on my shoulder like someone does to comfort. I cannot recall exactly what was being said, as I was a child and unfamiliar with what they were doing. Yet as I go back through the memory of my mind to what I know now I think it was most likely a pronouncement of time of death. I do remember someone saying something about the time. I watched the fireman and emergency workers as they started putting things away. I remember looking at the people that were present as they brought my dad out on a gurney. He was fully covered with a white sheet.

What does my story about losing a father have to do with me stepping into my power at work or anyplace else?

My father had died on a Sunday. I went back to school on Monday. At that time our schools were not up to speed on the research and literature of social and psychological welfare of children as they are today. I remember several of my classmates who lived nearby and knew my father. They showed care in the ways children do. They asked about him. I remember how Billy put his arm around me for consolation. We went outside to play together and that was pretty much it as for as school was concerned.

I was a good student as most of the children in my class were as well. I excelled academically and recreationally and prided myself for always being one of the first girls picked for teams. At the end of the school year was the awards assembly. I was proud to receive the perfect attendance award from my teacher for not missing a day of class for the entire school year although my dad had just died that spring.

The days and years to come would go on pretty much in the same manner as they did before; I had good school performance, received awards and acknowledgements, and just stayed busy with lots of play and extracurricular activity.

The trauma was there unacknowledged, unattended, and intact.

I had learned how to accommodate and make space in my body for pain, disbelief, and uncertainty. I had learned how to manage my emotions carefully and without incidence so to continue staying on track and doing what needed to be done. I had learned how to internalize the most egregiously painful experience and almost pretend like it never happened. After I completed college, this behavior became my modus operandi as a young professional and eventual executive woman of color.

I share my story of trauma with you to illustrate how I learned to push through without ever thinking about the possibility that there were emotional blocks that would hold me back in unconscious ways. I learned (and am still learning) through therapeutic practice how much trauma I held in my body as a girl and carried into womanhood. I learned about competitive forms of performance and its role to manipulate the pain to continue meeting goals and exceeding expectations. I learned that I had to do good and be successful in my life to honor my dad and make things easier for my mom.

The problem with that is that I was on my own and that my success depended upon me. I hadn't learned how to get the care and support I needed from others around me. I needed my family and yet also wanted to be a good daughter that assumed self-leadership and didn't want to be a burden for my grieving mother. The only job she told me I had was to do well in school and get a good job. And that's exactly what I did.

I learned how to muster up the courage and strength required to plow through just about anything. School success. Completed. Land your first salaried position in management with health care, dental care, and vision benefits plus a 401K plan right out of college. Done. Drive your first brand new car right off the lot and get your first apartment without the need for a co-signer. Got that. You get the idea.

I never looked back. I carried the pain, disappointment, and fear of failure all the time. Yet, I had a well-developed mental capacity to seemingly compartmentalize so I could get done what I needed to do. Being a former student-athlete gave me the mental tools and physical stamina I needed to be strong and press forward when things got tough. Being a singer most of my life in choral groups gave me the social and performance instruments necessary, that I could access in order to stand upright and breathe properly, and to be ready to perform (i.e., talk) for an audience. I had developed the tools I needed and I had a track record of performance with grace and confidence.

More Trauma

I received word while I was living and working in Los Angeles that my mother had suffered a major stroke. I traveled home to Stockton to gather with the family. Upon arrival at the hospital, I was able to see my mother and talk with her. I noted how the left side of her face had sunken downward and how her speech was slurred. Yet she was smiling when I entered her room and she was able to talk with me. She asked me about Judy and wanted to know where she was. Judy was the older sister right above me and she wasn't at the hospital with us.

Within a few seconds my other sister had pulled me into a waiting room. She told me that they received word that Judy had been killed in an automobile accident in Sacramento right after leaving the hospital the evening before. As I was driving from Los Angeles, my sister waited for me to arrive before sharing this horrible news.

While in the waiting room, mom's doctor and more medical staff came in. Her doctor asked if I was the last daughter to arrive and after that was confirmed he went on to say that I couldn't say anything to my mother about what happened to our sister. We could not show emotion around mom because her condition was already fragile. Her doctor had forbidden the family to tell my mother about the tragedy of her daughter who had left her side just hours earlier to go drop off the kids, pick up fresh clothes, and return to the hospital.

My sister was forty years old at the time of her death and the mother of three children. All three of her children were present in the car during the accident. Fortunately, none were hurt. Her autopsy report said she had died immediately upon blunt impact. Her eldest son, my nephew Eli, served as a protective barrier so his younger sister and younger brother wouldn't have to see their mom while waiting on Interstate-5 for emergency personnel. Eli was fifteen years old at the time.

Three days after my sister's accident my mother had a sudden turn for the worse and we rushed back to the hospital advised that her condition now was touch and go. We learned that during the early morning hours my mother had overheard nurses outside her room talking about my sister as the tragedy made the local news. Several nurses had met my sister at the hospital as she had been the first family attendee to be with my mother after her stroke just days before.

My mother learned through their conversation the reason why her daughter had not returned to the hospital. She had been expecting her to come right back and was becoming agitated to not have a good reason. Mom went into near respiratory failure and other complications. Her recovery thereafter was long and tedious. Mom's spirit never was the same in my view. We buried my sister. I went back to work in Los Angeles.

Moving to San Francisco and Coming Home

I had wanted to move closer to home for some time and when the opportunity finally came, I took an appointment to become a dean at a university in San Francisco. I had loved my years in Los Angeles yet knew it was time to come home. San Francisco proved to be a special place to be both personally and professionally. I met and married my husband. There would be more acknowledgement, an executive appointment by the San Francisco mayor, and recognition from the business and local community for the good work I was putting forth into the world on the diversity and inclusion front.

All the while my heart remained broken and only got worse after my mom's stroke and my sister's passing.

Stepping into your power is the final step in guiding your transformation. This work is always about becoming your true and highest self as a woman of color leader. I could not become that woman until I could break through the broken-heartedness of my losses. Leadership for women of color is an act of loving others. The highest service I can give to my students and women in my life is to freely and openly listen and share. The highest service I can give to you is to freely and openly share my story, in hope that you might be able to identify and connect with the trauma that can hold you back from yourself, from your leadership, from your power.

My healing has only begun and will continue for years to come. I found my power and I am stepping into it because I see my trauma and no longer pretend it doesn't exist. You will become that woman of leadership and influence as you fulfill this step in your process.

I want to leave you with three ideas to enhance your leadership:

- Stepping into your power comes when you know what matters most. Prioritize your health and wellness above all else, and other gifts will flow thereafter.
- Stepping into your power is an acceptance to your calling; your vocation; your destiny. If not you, who? If not now, when?
- Stepping into your power is when you realize that you are the only one who can make things better for the people you care about.

Practical Ways to Step into Your Power: Place the Bet on Yourself

Do your best to avoid giving others a reason to hold you back from the future position you deserve and were destined for. I advise all women I work with to invest in themselves first if they are able to, before they make investment in others.

If you have not done so already, take an assessment of what credentials you will need in the professional path you have chosen to ensure you reach the highest level of achievement that your field offers. Basically, make sure you are not rejected or excluded due to lack of a credential that's expected in your field. I essentially want to make sure you get to where you want to go. As a woman of color in leadership, expect that you will not be extended a pass in this area (unless you or your family owns the company or you start your own). And even if that is the case, for purposes of ensuring the due respect in your chosen field, you may still want to get all the necessary credentials and professional certifications.

If a job or career has traditionally required an advanced degree, or a certain certificate, you will be held to the standard of having it complete and in place. Place the bet on yourself first. Make the investment in your continued education and identify the support you need to get it done.

Defy Expectations

Defying others' expectations is nothing new to you. One of the greatest motivators throughout my life was blasting through and beyond the low expectations that others would place upon me. There's nothing like proving success by surpassing what others have said you would not be; there is a particular sadness when their support could have made for a collective celebration. You were made to push past and beyond others' tepid and thin expectations.

Know that when I talk about defying expectations, I am talking about going beyond what others may place upon you. Think about defying the expectations and reconsidering the (initial) goals you may have set for yourself. Many women of color I work with have stepped into their power and are going far beyond what they have initially planned for their lives. Your opportunity and success bar, really, is set and accomplished only by you.

Identify and Use the Tools at Your Disposal

One thing to remember is that your power is not always apparent to others, especially when your title or position does not support the traditional notion of power. Due to the hierarchal nature of work, people respond much differently to the title "president" than they would to say, "director." Yet, you can cultivate and nurture your power in a position or role that has a less influential or traditionally powerful role, and still be a powerful woman of color at work.

How do you become powerful when you are not in one of the most senior roles in your organization?

Identify the tools that are within your reach that give you the advantage to make an impact. You can do this from where you are right now. For instance, how much flexibility do you have in your role? If you are flexible, create a business reason to collaborate and work with others you admire or those who you want to eventually work for. Become known in the organization as a collaborator and new opportunities will emerge.

You may have more tangible tools at your disposal than you think, like being able to make decisions on who gets to be on a workgroup or committee; or being in charge of making decisions about who gets to serve on a special taskforce or what initiatives will receive special funding if you have the budget decision authority. Maybe your influence decides what projects get launched and when. All of these examples are more than workplace inertia. It's critically important for women of color to recognize all of the assets that are in your leadership quiver to become more creative and intentional in advancing your success as well as the success of others.

Be Strategic with Gender and Race

For as much as progress that has been made, with men and women of color advancing in all facets of American professional life and with the election of the first African American president, still bad habits die hard. Even new, futuristic, and "young" industries present evidence that the seeds of societal discrimination remain and permeate into the DNA of even the newest of economic endeavors. Yet, women of color have been left out and left behind for too long and now important people are noticing this fact.

Be Strategic to Be in the Right Place at the Right Time

The New Yorker published a letter from Silicon Valley in its November 20, 2017, issue titled "The Tech Industry's Gender-Discrimination Problem." This particular article discusses Google and Tesla's discrimination in hiring practices and brings to light the gender and racial makeup of Google's workforce. Google only published its data in 2014 after tremendous public pressure. Of its technical staff, only 17% were women, Hispanics 2%, and African Americans 1%, improving slightly after its third diversity report in June 2017, to 20, 3, and 1 percents, respectively. In April 2017, the Department of Labor found "systemic compensation disparities against women pretty much across the entire workforce." Here is an example of a modern high-tech company that systematically hires fewer women, fewer Hispanics, fewer African Americans and pays them less across the board. Pretty damning evidence for a modern company, which is also a financial powerhouse.

Tech companies are known to be slow in the hiring of women and minorities for senior positions. Finally, in July 2017, Tesla welcomed Ebony Media's CEO, Linda Johnson Rice to its nine-member board of directors... she's one of only two women and the first African American according to Fortune.

In 2017, three Latina engineers sued Uber Technologies for discriminating against female employees and both men and women of color, citing compensation practices and the employee ranking system which allegedly favors men and white or Asian employees.

A 2018 meta-analysis, which is a larger study of several studies, published in the *Journal of Applied Psychology* demonstrates the challenges for women and people of color. An increase in woman of color representation is not a satisfactory solution alone to systemic discrimination. More women of color must accede to decision-making positions and to the C-suite to improve the system. This type of systemic disease cannot be cured with an aspirin or a Band-Aid. The system needs an overhaul.

The systemic ways to exclude women of color have been practiced and mastered by organizations through the individuals who lead them. However, the days of blatant exclusion and oversight of the immensely talented pool of women of color are showing signs of societal discomfort and rejection—for the good of everyone.

Be ready to step into your power as the time is nigh.

Chapter 10

Crushing the Impostor Syndrome

W hen I was a dean of students, I noticed a pattern in the reports from staff members who worked closely with the new students. By the sixth week into the new semester, some students reported feelings of discomfort on campus. They were having a difficult time adjusting to university life overall. They didn't get along with their new dormitory roommate. They hadn't connected with their professors. They were not sure if they had made a mistake and picked the wrong university.

In doing follow-up or intervention work with the faculty, I discovered a pattern. The perception of the student didn't always align with what their faculty member thought or what their roommate experienced with the student. Picking the right university takes time—and I always gave preference to the students' wisdom about what was going on. Sometimes it was clear to others that the student was struggling. I was more concerned about my students' lack of a sense of belonging.

My experience taught me that with the right set of conditions, a great faculty mentor, meaningful social engagement with peers, accessible academic support including writing and tutoring, most students will get through the rocky transition phase and remain through four years. There were students, though, who asked questions about themselves that did not sit well with me.

"I'm not sure I belong here" came up enough with students of color that in time I came to believe that there were things we needed to do better to make the campus a welcoming environment and second home for them. I'd work on finding ways to make the campus feel like a place they belonged. However, I also felt there was more going on there.

It seemed as if the students were doubting their presence on campus in general for more than wrong university fit; and that it was about whether or not they should even be attending the school itself. I accepted that we had work to do on making sure the campus felt like home for all students. And there was something more going on that was centered on the students' perception of themselves and their capacities to be successful. I learned about Impostor Syndrome during my counseling education and social justice studies master's program. I became concerned that my students were experiencing Impostor Syndrome.

What Is Impostor Syndrome?

Coined and identified in 1978 by two leading female psychologists, Dr. Pauline R. Clance and Dr. Suzanne A. Imes, Impostor Syndrome is defined as an individual experience of self-perceived intellectual phoniness and fraud despite evidence of high achievement. ("The Imposter Phenomenon in High Achieving Women: Dynamics and therapeutic intervention" in *Psychotherapy: Theory, Research & Practice*, vol.15 n.3 1978 pp.241-247)

Another way of looking at Impostor Syndrome is hinted at in the title of this book. It does not matter what you have accomplished. Even though you have worked twice as hard and you've become twice as good, it may still not be enough even when all the evidence proves otherwise.

Impostor Syndrome initially described the experiences of white women who believed their achievements were a result of happenstance; who lived in fear of being taken as a fraud, and setting sometimes unrealistically high standards of achievement. This syndrome may be more exacerbated in people of color, particularly women, who often receive societal messages of not belonging or not being good enough. (Cokely, K., et. al., 2013.)

I noticed when my students communicated thoughts to me that suggested they were experiencing some level of the impostor phenomena. I recognized a pattern among students of color, especially the undergraduates. Too many of them in my opinion.

There are a multitude of issues that a dean of students deals with at a university or college campus, Impostor Syndrome frequently being one of them. Here are three of the most common and persistent questions that came up in my conversations with students that indicate the feeling of being an impostor:

Do I Really Belong Here?
Am I good enough?
Am I a fraud?

Feelings and sensitivity about one's achievement are not unusual. Everyone is susceptible to wanting a sense of belonging and feeling like they matter where they are located. My point was the prevalence of these mental states and self-ideation thoughts among Black/African

American, Latina, Asian American, Indigenous, Pacific Islander and women students overall.

Part of my work was to make note of contexts so I could assess how to best support the student and see what intervention or strategy to consider. The environment of the campus was the first context to examine, to see if there was an environmental condition that created even more stress during the first six weeks and entire first semester transition phase.

What campus environmental factors can we attribute to the student's difficult transition? If the student was feeling singled out or targeted in the classroom, was it related to their identity? How is the roommate relationship issue being handled by the residence hall staff? Is the student eating and sleeping? Have they made friends?

These targeted questions are part of the quiver of tools that a dean uses to gather information to ensure student success. I learned over time that one of the most important things I could work on was creating experiences for students that engendered a strong sense of belonging from the moment they arrived—to not only tell my students they were welcome, but be responsive in creating experiences that demonstrated we cared about them. The purpose was to make sure they felt that the campus was their home too.

This person-centered approach sought to counter the lack of belonging through finding ways to connect students to others and build community. It's through the sense of community that students become rooted, make meaning of what's going on around them, and find their way in a new campus community. As feelings of doubt began to dissipate, it was because they were in relationships with others. They found relationships where others saw them.

They became visible to others, which promoted even more interpersonal engagement and more relationships. Feelings of insecurity, doubt, and fear were replaced with security, affiliation, and belonging.

My goal was to create a sense of place where my students felt that they were known by others, that they were seen and heard, and that they were cared for and loved by the university. The campus was their new home and we were their extended family.

Impostor Syndrome and Women of Color

Do I really belong here?

It's a mental threat to a woman of color. It's a threat to enacting her leadership and will prevent her from stepping into her power.

Women of color share with me real instances when others at work actually made them feel that they did not belong. Comments made directly or indirectly sometimes from co-workers, other times verbal slights by their peers. These reports of microaggressions only strengthen one's concern about belonging. Even women of color who have a strong sense of their identity, and who are not easily rattled or intimidated sometimes are impacted by the internalized and wrong perception of fraudulence that Impostor Syndrome exposes. In my view, the students of color or the professional women of color did not bring a mental condition with them. The state they felt and discussed with trusted advisors was the accumulation of gender and racial social pressure. The collection of thoughts they carried were part of what happens from being emotionally fatigued by the forces of racism and misogyny.

I was concerned the mental blocks that emerged from Impostor Syndrome were formed and reinforced by unconscious, yet real messages students and professionals of color were receiving from others about their performance and worth.

The interesting thing is that impostor syndrome goes beyond the lives of students. Once formed, the Impostor Syndrome follows us, women of color, throughout our professional lives and can become a mental block and, worse, a barrier to our success. Professional women of color describe the same instances of slights and implicit bias in the workplace that can produce the same mental block associated with Impostor Syndrome that I heard about (and still hear about) from undergraduate students.

I see Impostor Syndrome as a threat to women of color. It is a lie that probably came straight from hell. Impostor Syndrome is absolutely not true.

This is an important message for you because, like my students, you will experience interactions at work that suggest or tell you that you are an impostor. This will only reinforce the self-inflicted thoughts and ideation of not being good enough. You have already worked twice as hard at everything you do to be where you are.

People already know your worth but won't tell you. This can make you feel like you still do not belong. Some women of color report the audacity of co-workers who engage in microaggressions—everyday slights in a covert manner without concern of retribution. The point is to have strategies ready to deal with Impostor Syndrome when it comes at you so that it doesn't get in your head.

How to Crush Impostor Syndrome

One of the ways you can crush Impostor Syndrome is being aware that it's real and exists. Impostor Syndrome is a real mental block in the mental health literature that has been studied and researched. Learn how to recognize it when it shows up for you. You will need to be mindful of stressors that trigger a thought of not belonging so that you may usurp these negative thoughts and replace them with an actual account of what's really going on for you.

Finding your community is the most important thing you can do to counteract the occurrence of Impostor Syndrome. Your community takes the form of affinity groups and being with others who have similar identity as your own, gender and race, who may also be going through some of the same social experiences at work.

Affinity groups or sister circles are the place to be vulnerable and open about your experience as a woman of color. The isolation you feel as a woman of color only adds to Impostor Syndrome. Having a community around shared identity and experiences will allow you to see yourself in relation to the strength of the community itself; and the shared identity strengthens the group itself and what they bring and offer to the organization.

Fellowship with other women of color is necessary and fundamental to combat Impostor Syndrome.

Check in with your transformative allies when you are experiencing Impostor Syndrome and find a way to let them know about problems you are experiencing at work. As an advocate for you, they care about your overall sense of inclusion and when there is a problem. A transformative ally's support is critical as they will remind you of your worth and value to the organization when an interpersonal situation leaves you feeling that you do not belong.

The key to crushing the Impostor Syndrome is be clear that you are meant to be where you are. You have the right to be. Spend time with people who remind you who you are. Find and associate with people who affirm you and your identity. People who know your worth, contribution, and value.

You are greatly needed in your organizational environment and what you bring makes a difference. There isn't anyone with your unique perspective. That is what makes women of color in leadership special in the workplace.

Conclusion

T he first time I can recall the *Twice as Good* advisement, I was
eleven years old and my father had passed away about a year
earlier. I could not understand at the time what *Twice as Good*
meant. Nearly every African American woman I have met over the years
has a similar story of when she first heard this cautionary tale of how the
world would receive us, and pre-emptive instruction on what we needed
to do to be ready and respond accordingly.

Twice as Good is an intersectional leadership framework I've prepared
for women of color who want to be taken seriously as leaders on their
terms, yet who face invisible and real barriers against their success at
work. The title of this book is inspired by my own experience, from
receiving parental guidance urging me to do better and excel even more
in school when I wanted to spend more time playing outside.

In this work the focus is at the intersection of gender and race
and the unique ways in which that intersection shows up every day
for women of color in leadership. It's at the intersection of gender and

race where women of color discover and step into their power. You can find resources that focus on how to lean in to engage issues of gender in the workplace. Yet those works miss the sufficiently sophisticated or nuanced approach to leadership practice women of color need to be successful. The experiences that women of color face, the effects of misogyny and racism on a regular basis, are often unseen, invisible, and therefore overlooked.

Twice as Good is simple instruction within a complex, systemic reality of intersectionality given from a Black mother to her Black daughter, while also an indictment on what it means to be Black and female in America. I have found that women of color across diverse cultures, experiences, and ethnicities share my experience creating a collectivized understanding and community with Asian American, Latinas, Middle Eastern, Indigenous, and other women of color who share similar advisement from their families.

"You're going to have to work twice as hard, and be twice as good." That is a lot of pressure for a child to take on, yet that's exactly what I did for the sum of my career as an executive woman of color.

As a professor of leadership and a strategic diversity expert I share twenty-five years of experience on how to teach and prepare executives, as well as master's level business students and doctoral level education scholars, on how to lead from a place of authenticity and inclusivity. I've gathered stories and lessons learned from the thousands of individuals I have taught and coached to provide their insight and perspective. In *Twice as Good*, I offer my signature 7-step process to become a disruptive, intersectional leader. This is a form of transformational leadership suited for the experiences and strengths of women of color. This work focuses on the distinct intersectional identities of gender and race and the culturally informed power women of color bring to leadership.

In this remarkable time of change, women of color are being called to align their personal power and cultural identity into their leadership.

Twice as Good is a culturally-informed strategy to work against structural inequity at work and in society. Using storytelling and narrative as a form of leadership development and personal experiences as a model for leadership practice, I cull the lessons learned on how gender and race come together in the workplace to create tremendous opportunity and value for organizations everywhere.

Today I understood my mother's instruction to always do more as not only a strategy for her child facing disadvantage in society, but her instruction was also a critique on how the country regarded me as a Black child who would grow into a Black woman.

I embraced her advisement from a place of gratitude for her love to protect me from social oppression by committing to personal excellence as a form of resistance. Yet, I too resist the notion of individual responsibility alone to counteract or personally remedy the deep, structural, and unfair social inequity that exists by simply doing more or doing better. Due to a deliberate and sustained collective failure of leadership that was outside of my control and responsibility, misogyny and racism remain rampant and still exist today.

This book will serve as a leadership guide through everyday issues you will face as a woman of color in a leadership role at your work. This book is a transformation and empowerment tool as you confront and manage unconscious bias and microaggressions, and build inclusivity within your organization or corporate entity. Whether you work in government or for a corporation, *Twice as Good* will be your go-to guide to work through leadership challenges, and will remind you how to find and when to activate your strengths.

If you completed the book, you have learned to be more confident in how you show up. You understand how to be conscious in your identities as a source of power, competence, and leadership advantage in whatever endeavor you take on. You know the legacy of truth telling that women of color carry within them—this will embolden your voice as you speak truth to power. You will know how to find the right ally who will stand with you when you need them the most.

Now, not later, is the time for women of color to assume their rightful place in the pantheon of principled and mission-driven leaders who stepped into their power when it mattered most. You have a leadership story unfolding that is waiting to be told. Listen carefully to the world as it tells us what to do next through the stories of those who have been marginalized, made vulnerable, and left behind.

The intersectional leadership of women of color is for those who care for others deeply, wholeheartedly, while deploying a disruptive and reflective leadership practice at the same time.

I want to remind you that your leadership is intertwined with transformative allies who will be your partners to build a better workplace and a better world. It took a series of setbacks and significant social inequity over recent years to finally convince well-intended colleagues that race relations and gender equity is a problem at work and in our communities. New found awareness is a positive outcome to the more recent equality set-backs. Awareness and consciousness provides allies the opportunity to move beyond an overly simplistic and trite understanding of race and gender issues so they can become a true ally for you. Transformative allyship is tremendously hard work. Yet it must be done. I am convinced that you are the right person leading where you are at this moment. Your organization needs you to offer new perspectives and new narratives for new solutions. Or your next appointment or opportunity is waiting for you to step into your leadership.

We will build a more equitable and just world through the leadership of women of color in partnership with their transformative allies.

This is your call to action to learn the principles in *Twice as Good* and to integrate them into your leadership practice at work. As you commit to the way of greater consciousness in how to become the leader who changes the narrative on what's possible at work, I encourage you to support others along the way, especially women of color within your reach who need a grounded, purpose-driven leader to support and mentor them. Bring others along as you rise and ascend. Leadership is why you are here and inclusive power is what you are made for.

Acknowledgements

This book has been on my mind and in my heart for much longer than it took for me to write. When it came time to sit down and allow it to come forth into the world, I was only able to do so with the love and support of family and friends.

First, I am grateful to my brilliant and loving daughters for their guidance and support on this project. I couldn't have done this work without Hannah and Naomi giving me their reflections and feedback. I am grateful for the insightful conversations we had together to clarify what I wanted to say in this book as millennial women of color at the beginning of their beautiful lives.

I am grateful to the gifted and caring team of the University of San Francisco's Diversity Engagement and Community Outreach Office (DECO), who are a home away from home for inspiration and community.

I have been blessed to have many diverse and remarkable persons who have entered my life. They have left their imprint with me. These persons have supported and believed in me, whether they were up close or far in the distance. I want to try to name and acknowledge some of you: Cortes Saunders, Janice Mirikitani, Cecil Williams, Kathy Nitchoff, Jussara Souza, Donal Godfrey, Jeanie Madsen, Camille Jordan, Julia Dowd, Clarence Jones, Antoinette Malveaux, Ed Schoenberg, Sammy Hoi, Rhonda Magee, Shabnam Koirala-Azad, Barbara Avery, Ava Ward, Jennifer Turpin, Eva Monroe, Kaye Foster, Hydra Mendoza, Marcelo Camperi, Fabienne McPhail-Naples, Bob Naples, Ennette Morton, Bill Hing, Maisha Beasley, Leonora Flores, Sabrina Sanders, Francine Martinez, Susan Mitchell, Tyrone Cannon, Susan Koret, Karen Nicholson, Betty Taylor, Carolina Cárdenas, Troy Cole, Kieu Vo, John Trasviña, Patricia Mitchell, Michael Pappas, Elena Flores, Cassandra Moreno, Angie Nakamoto, Auoie Rubio, Rachel James, Allison Dumas, Judy Karshmer, Peter Novak, Noah Borrero, Art Torres, LaSchaunda Smaw, Salvador Aceves, Luis Herrera, Liz Davis, Diane Woods, Skye Patrick, Adriana Broullon, Christine Yeh, Alex Gonzalez, Margaret Higgins, Steve Privett, James Taylor, Tracy Porter, Joe Marshall, Chuck Smith, Monetta White, Nancy Cantor, Susan Christian and Ria DasGupta. And in memory to those who invested in my future who have transitioned—Gerardo Marin, Ed Lee, Andy Thompson, Sandra Kuchler, Joseph White, John LoSchiavo and my parents Mary and James.

I am grateful for my mother's sister, Aunt Hattie, who encourages me on a weekly basis reminding me who I am and from whom I've come through; that is everything. Thank you for being a mother for me. And finally, to my partner, David. You have patiently and lovingly walked beside me and at times behind me—where I need you most on this journey. Thank you for loving me, looking after my needs, and having my back.

To the Morgan James Publishing team: Special thanks to David Hancock, CEO & Founder for believing in me and my message. To my Author Relations Manager, Margo Toulouse, thanks for making the process seamless and easy. Many more thanks to everyone else, but especially Jim Howard, Bethany Marshall, and Nickcole Watkins.

About the Author

 Known as the diversity and inclusion expert for mission-driven organizations, Dr. Mary J. Wardell is an educator, author, executive, and thought leader on implementing broad-based and equitable diversity strategies that work. Dr. Wardell is a diversity and inclusion expert who understands the unique duty of leaders to advance social justice, love, and inclusivity in their organizations. She has served as the inaugural vice provost and chief diversity and community engagement officer at the University of San Francisco (USF) since 2011 and is a leadership, organizations, and diversity studies lecturer in the USF School of Education and USF School of Management. She was the Dean of Students from 2008-2011 and co-founded with student activists the Gender and Sexuality Student Resources Center at the University of San Francisco. Mary received the Most Influential Woman award by the San Francisco Business Times in

2017 and won the 2018 Human Rights award by the Committee on the Elimination of Discrimination Against Women (CEDAW) and the 2015 San Francisco Human Rights Commission Hero Award. Dr. Wardell is the Founder of Latinas in Leadership, an empowerment conference and leadership movement for Chicanx-Latinx leaders.

Mary serves as the President of the San Francisco Public Library Commission stewarding $160M budget for a system of twenty-eight city public libraries. Under her leadership, the San Francisco Public Library won the coveted National Public Library of the Year in 2018. She is also a trustee for the National Urban Libraries Council, Washington, D.C, the Ignatian Solidarity Network, Washington, D.C., and the San Francisco Interfaith Council. A past dean of student affairs at Otis College of Art and Design in Los Angeles and former assistant dean of students at California State University, San Marcos, Dr. Wardell is the Founder and Principal of The DEI Leadership Group, a diversity solutions, leadership development and crisis management firm in San Francisco.

During the Great Migration, her parents journeyed from rural Arkansas and Texas to the South-side of Stockton, California, a vibrant, multicultural community where she was born and reared with her sisters. She resides in San Francisco with her husband and daughters. This is her first book. Dr. Mary J. Wardell is available for select readings and lectures. To inquire about an appearance, contact at Mary@ Deileadershipgroup.com.

Thank You

Thank you for allowing me to guide you on your leadership journey. I truly appreciate the trust that you placed in my efforts, and I hope that this book has given you the faith and courage to step into your leadership now, and not later, giving you wisdom and strategies to use to disrupt the status quo in organizations and bring intersectional leadership into practice.

I understand there was information in the book you may want to learn. That is why I created companion learning experience, *The Twice as Good Leadership Mastermind*. This is an experiential engagement for people who prefer learning in community how to leverage an intersectional leadership framework offered in *Twice as Good*. Available in on-line and face to face formats, I build on the principles of the book with a focus on social justice, inclusivity, and being wholehearted in everything you do.

If you individually, or with a small team of leaders you work closely with, are ready to step into your power and hope to work with me on building your diversity and leadership capacities, then feel free to contact for a strategy session. Simply go to www.DEILeadershipGroup.com.

(DEI—Diversity, Equity, Inclusion).

#TwiceAsGoodTheBook

Printed in the USA
CPSIA information can be obtained
at www.ICGtesting.com
JSHW082351140824
68134JS00020B/2013